S0-DXN-337

Engaging the Aging in Ministry

by Mark Bergmann and Elmer Otte

CONCORDIA

Publishing House
St. Louis

ALFRED AND CAROL BASTIN

Copyright © 1981
Concordia Publishing House
3558 South Jefferson Avenue
St. Louis, Missouri 63118

Manufactured in the United States of America

Library of Congress Cataloging in Publication Data

Bergmann, Mark, 1926-
        Engaging the aging in ministry.

        1. Church work with the aged. 2. Aged—Religious life. I. Otte, Elmer, joint author.
II. Title.
BV4435.B4   259'.3   81-314
ISBN 0-570-03833-2

                                                                    AACR1

1   2   3   4   5   6   7   8   9   10   PP PP   90   89   88   87   86   85   84   83   82   81

Contents

Contents

Introduction

There is a growing awareness of the aging in all sectors of society, and no less in the church. This is evident in the large number of programs being developed for this rapidly expanding segment of society. More and more the pastoral ministry is also occupied (and often preoccupied) with the special needs of this age group.

Well-developed and -organized programs are available nationally and regionally—also within the church. Some of them can be readily adapted to local situations. Others must be used in connection with nationally or organizationally administered programs. Some of the major secular and religious programs and the headquarters from which information may be obtained are listed in the bibliographical data in the back of this resource.

If elaborate programs for the aged are already available, why then this manual? We have discovered that there are as yet very few Christian church programs that go beyond offering services *to* and *for* the elderly to engage them in ministry. The retired population (of which only 5 percent are in nursing homes) constitutes a large pool of spiritual power and talents as well as life skills that lie untapped by the church simply because the local congregation does not know where to begin engaging the aging in ministry. This manual then is offered as a means of launching a senior ministry geared to the individual resources and conditions of the local church. The guidelines in this book can be followed as a way of activating and involving that reservoir of gifts God has given and nurtured for the growth of His people and to serve many of the needs society and the church are too short-handed to supply.

As with all manuals, the suggestions herein do not apply to all situations, but there are enough choices to fit groups of any size or makeup. The local pastor or congregational leader, following the guidelines and consulting the resources here presented, can help the elderly of the church develop a program of their own that will make them feel useful and will employ their mature and unique talents for the good of others. The professional ministers of the church can use this manual to guide the aging population in setting up and administering their own program, but it will achieve its designed purpose most successfully if it becomes an early handbook for the elderly themselves as members of planning committees and as lay leaders.

The manual contains suggestions for services *to* the aging as well as encouragement for participation in national and regional programs. These services *for* the aging can be used as a means of training them for service. Make it the aim of your local group or individuals to move themselves to the point where the program is theirs. This should be done as soon as possible, beginning with the very planning for a ministry of the aging. For, as Elmer Otte never tires of saying: "The program is not theirs until they own it."

Drawing upon their extensive personal experience and a vast array of resources, the authors herewith provide the tools and a set of instructions for a lively and productive ministry of the aging.

Chapter I

Retirement and Attendant Changes During the Aging years

Retirement, in our society, is an expected reality. Most persons do retire, and they are expected to experience this disengagement from life's career work—whether they are willing or ready or whether they resist and fear being out of work, out of a paycheck, and out of their familiar roles of usefulness and importance.

Until recently, more than half took their social security at age 62. Historically, workers "had to" retire at age 65. A recent law change permits some workers to stay on until age 70 if employer and worker can work it out and if the worker is still useful.

However, not everyone is happy with all the experiences of retirement. Some workers (especially men) come home to a new life of nothing to do. Work and its structure was easier. The worker always knew where he had to be, when to be there; he knew what was expected of him—and how it was to be done. And he kept being reminded if he lapsed in his job.

Now he is free—free to do what he pleases. What happens all too often, if he doesn't get sick or die from what gerontologists call the syndrome of Age 66, is that he may give his spouse an ulcer—or worse.

This is called "being underfoot." Always monitoring, watching, suggesting better ways of doing things. The husband may not be aware that this is really not "his place." The home is still the homemaker's place of business. Even if the female did retire from her own career job, she still has her traditional role to play at home. If the phone rings, chances are the call is for her.

These changes can set up tensions, especially if candid dialog and preplanning did not get done. There continues to be a serious lack of planning for living one's later years. Someone, the church for example, should make of this a vital ministry.

How About This Parish and Its Job Clearinghouse?

Sure, your aging are retired; they have had their career burdens and do not wish to get all that involved again. Well, there is a parish in Kokomo, Indiana, where they list odd jobs that need doing in the parish area. Some are tasks which a widow lady cannot do or get done, and she is seeking help. Some are mini-career things through which a willing guy can still pick up a few dollars.

Lists posted in the parish hall state what jobs need doing;

things like window washing, putting on or taking off storm windows; spading up a small garden; checking out some simple lamp not lighting, or shorted electric cord problems, things like that. Frequently it is no more than helping to secure a door that is not locking very well, or a sink that needs unplugging; jobs which do not require true tradesmen help. What a practical parish ministry which helps where people hurt!

While relationships during the early time of retirement may take some adjusting, there should be a systematic "getting out of the house," most especially by the male spouse, but also by each party. They need not always, and only, go together. There are fortunate persons who are so sufficiently self-actualized that they know where they are going; they pretty well keep control over their own choices. For them and their spouses there is more fun and excitement and less tension.

Which Is Cause and Which Is Effect?

Even when retirement becomes reality, how it is viewed by individuals and families can differ widely. Check the validity of the following statements:
- Retirement is God's, and society's, gift of free time.
- Retirement is a highly individual circumstance; it is, usually, either a problem or an opportunity.
- Retirement is, finally, largely an attitudinal situation.
- Retirement, for society, is a vast and mostly untapped potential for good; 25 million skilled and experienced persons, most with wisdom and judgment to share.

We, who carry some of the responsibility for the aging, must take note of all that needs to be done in our world and all that could be done by this array of talent. Until now, most of us have not known where to begin, or whether to bother.

A Starting Point: Enlighten Their Self-Concern

To begin with, older persons must be reminded of simple, basic health facts. Research shows that those who look forward to the years of their aging will probably live longer. They are also most apt to remain vital and useful, avoiding and postponing senility which need not be inevitable. Note: Ninety-five percent of older persons do not become senile, and further, they do not end up moving to a nursing home. Since that good news is statistically true, then we in the church have a vast army of members to minister to, a large potential to draw into new and exciting ministries of serving each other, of helping still others.

Doctors press the point: Older persons must keep their weight down; they should exercise regularly, and stop smoking. They should learn to direct their stresses—into the all-embracing hands of Almighty God, and then they ought to direct their minds to active and person-involving pursuits.

ACTION SUGGESTIONS/FOR WORKING AT WELLNESS
Work at Staying Fit
- *Walk two ways*—one, a stride-out, feeling good walk to get

some place, to get oxygen pumping into your blood; two, walk instead of riding; on elevators you ride, on stairs you walk. Walk, walk, walk.

- *Stretch*—for feeling good, for loosening up, for toning muscles, for working tightness and kinks.
- *Keep active*—keep busy; avoid nibbling instead of eating regular meals; keep weight down so your heart does not have all that fatty tissue to pump blood through.
- *Try sports-type activity*—for the fun of the game, for getting vigorous exercise, for competing with others—within reason of course.

Avoid What Can Only Hurt

- Skip the drug habit unless required by specific ailments, doctor's orders (one exception: keep high blood pressure controlled, by living more calmly, more sensibly, and by prescribed medical means. Another exception: diabetes.)
- Simply stop smoking; no if, ands, or buts.
- Cool it on drinking; especially do not mix alcohol and those drugs which interact.

Enjoy Eating Right, and Light

- Eat balanced meals from the four essential food groups: whole grains; fruits and vegetables (fresh when you can); protein foods including lighter, unfatty meats; and dairy products. Try drinking decaffeinated coffee; it's better for you.
- Work toward substituting unsaturated for animal fat spreads. Cut back on refined sugars, and cut back on salt.

  (Parish Seniors Committees: Bring in utility company home experts; dieticians; doctors and/or nurses to demonstrate and encourage alone persons to take better care of themselves.)

It Helps to Recognize Changes Which Aging Brings:

- *Physical change:* less awareness of feeling; a weakening of motor control; also less control of bladder, bowel, eating, chewing, swallowing.
- *Mental change:* a letdown in organization of affairs; less sureness about what to do in time of emergency or need; memory lapses and loss.
- *Psychosocial change:* concealing unfavorable appearances, if these have been harmed; letting go of independence; feelings of guilt and confusion; and a questioning of: "Why did God permit this to happen to me?"

Spiritual Well-Being: How the Wellness Theory Relates to It

Consider providing a theological affirmation on the Scriptural considerations of the whole person. Much data is available through denominational hospital groups and from church sources. It should be harnessed to meet some of the needs of older persons. Any agenda for action should include the family, the congregation, regional church groupings, and other institutions of the supportive and healing church.

All persons have worth and dignity, and this includes the elderly. All segments of the church should enlist their members, and their societies and structures, to involve the faithful in special and promising ministries to older persons. The early church was committed to preach, teach, and serve, and to provide a concerned-for-one-another fellowship. It may be time to consider a theology of aging to help guide us.

ACTION SUGGESTIONS/NOT WHAT YOU'RE EATING— WHAT'S EATING YOU

Manage Natural Stress

- Stress in life is natural; it puts zip and zest into our days. But, some stress is heavier, and harmful. The trick is how we respond to the stress that hits us.
- Avoid anxiety-boosting people, situations, and habits. Have faith, think up, and skip dwelling on the downside. Get good rest, not too little and not too, too much. Be nicer to yourself; you are older and this should be your golden time; let the golden glow shine through.
- Worry and fear are useless. God's love and protection are available. Learn to trust.

Play It Safe—Stay Sound

- Be alert to first aid needs potential; know where the first aid kit is kept. Slow down and try not to be clumsy.
- Use car seatbelts; lock car doors; keep theft bait out of tempting sight.
- Do not drive when you are not competent, when conditions, your own or the car's or the road's, are not first rate.
- Brush teeth on all four sides, front, back, and between; brush after eating, drinking sweets, carbohydrates; and floss regularly; remember to get to your dentist regularly.

How Are You Getting Along?

- You could have urgent need for your neighbors, and they can be a pleasant comfort at any time. Know them.
- Are you living enough of your daily life in the lives of others; living mostly outside of your own worries?
- Volunteer organizations need more good volunteers; mostly they need caring, concerned, happy-hearted persons. Try it.
- Keep making new, and if you can, younger friends. Stay friend-equipped.

(Parish Seniors Committee: Professional social workers, psychiatrists, counselors, are available to speak.)

Losses and Other Special Concerns of the Elderly:

Death and grief as an encounter; these often become too much a preoccupation of the elderly. There is learning needed here. Friends, family, neighbors will become ill, and may eventually die. Also, we may move, or they may, to the Sunbelt or across the country to be nearer to children.

Most older persons have trouble finding their way through the stages in the dying process; either in their own dying or in the terminal time of family members and others. The stages, as a reminder and for our understanding:

1. *Denial:* "No, not me." This response serves an important function: it allows the patient time to collect himself, and with time, he can mobilize other less radical defenses. Sometimes during this stage, patients will search for a doctor who will negate the diagnosis.

2. *Anger:* Denial eventually yields to deep anger. "Why me?" During this stage the patient is nasty, obnoxious, difficult, is never satisfied with nursing staff, medical care, or family. The more effective you are, the more you become the target of the hostility. Sometimes the staff retaliates by avoiding the patient or becoming angry in return.

3. *Bargaining:* Resentment is succeeded in turn by bargaining—a campaign, often undetectable, to somehow stay execution of sentence. A difficult patient may suddenly turn cooperative: the reward he seeks for good behavior is an extension of life. They bargain with God, with doctors, with themselves to have one more day without pain, one more chance to do something important, one more chance to attend a needed function.

4. *Depression:* After the bargaining stage, the patient sinks into a profound depression as he begins to face the reality of his death. The patient is weighing the fearful price of death, preparing himself to accept the loss of everything and everyone he loves. This leads to profound sadness and depression: a normal grief reaction to anticipated loss. It takes great courage and strength to face this loss and to express the grief. The patient needs help to cry and express sadness.

5. *Acceptance:* The fifth (and final) stage is acceptance, when at last the condemned patient bows to his sentence. Dr. Ross (who articulated these stages in her book, *Death and Dying)* feels this is a very peaceful, calm, beautiful time. One patient expressed it thus: "I think this is the miracle. I am ready now and am not even afraid anymore." She died the following day. These patients need little conversation and require only the touch of companionship or an almost silent support to keep them from feeling alone.

6. *Hope:* Dr. Ross feels that: (1) All terminally ill patients know they are dying—if you listen, they will tell you; (2) Hope is always there—in every stage. When a patient abandons hope, death is imminent; (3) It is not facing death that patients fear, but dying, a process almost as painful to see as to endure.

Losing a Spouse, or Losing a Friend or Family Member

It has been said that death is the ultimate terminal illness. Doctors remind us that we will probably die of one of four causes: heart attack, stroke, cancer, or as the result of an accident. They caution that we do not normally get to choose which our cause of death will be or when it shall visit us. Although God provides faith for all of life, it is most needed and most welcome at such inevitable times. Faith can and should be nurtured long before an emergency occurs. Why not enjoy that close relationship with God and take refuge in it when death comes?

Support Groups Make Difficult Recoveries Possible

In Wisconsin hospitals there are many specific ailment support groups: there are women who have had mastectomies who regularly visit and even demonstrate artifical replacement materials and methods for a missing breast. There are colostomy patients who are living normal lives and doing so happily. One such recovered patient we know goes (he is on call) to see new "ostomy" patients prior to surgery; he shows his own attachments, tells how they work, how they are cleansed and maintained. Patients who are filled with unspeakable fears take solace from what they learn from another person who had the same concerns.

One lady was so diligent about going to help others in such support groups that on the night she died her greatest regret was that she was going to miss that night's meeting and she would not be able to bring her encouragement anymore.

The Stages of Grief—and of Our Experience of Bereavement

1. *Shock:* Surviving family, friends, are usually thrown for a loop at the time of a loss. They suffer shock, they may protest with hostility, there may also be a denial. Many are filled with a profound fear at the loss of their (love) object.
2. *Disorganization:* In their despair, survivors suffer a kind of numbness, perhaps a disbelief; they exhibit a kind of restlessness; some even show signs of madness; they are searching.
3. *Violent emotions:* Anger and hostility are normal means of fighting back at what many grieving feel is unfair about their loss of a loved one. For many, there may be hostility toward family members or friends for a variety of real or imagined reasons—or without reason.
4. *Guilt:* It is not unusual for almost any of us to suffer feelings of guilt at the loss of a loved one. Who cannot dredge up thoughts of the times we were unkind, or neglectful, times we did not do all that we might have? Guilt is natural, but for some, discussion—or taking an action—can be helpful.
5. *Loss and loneliness:* Most of grief's reactions relate to, and keep coming back to, a fear of being denied, forevermore, the presence of the loved one; and it is clearly apparent that a great loneliness is bound—in many cases—to overwhelm. In time, outgoing action, relating to others, and a talking through, is often most helpful.
6. *Relief:* Grief, the reaction to the loss, is a process that must take place before acceptance. The involvement of community—a practice which many today

abhor and question—provides the opportunity for talking through, for sharing with others, that this loss is real, that it is heavy and sad, that it is not unusual, and that there are all these others who may each in his or her own way be supportive and comforting.

7. *Reestablishment:* Finally, there is the realization that the loss is being accepted—by community and by self. There comes the time, or the day, when the surviving person reorganizes. (One woman made a list of the things, the activities, she feared most doing by herself, now all alone. But, one by one, she started taking them on and doing them. Once she had done each one time, she felt stronger to go on doing these same dreaded activities.) Grief takes a lot of growing out of self.

The Elderly Need Reasons to Get Up Each Day

Joe retired in Minnesota's Twin Cities, sat down at home and listened to his arteries harden. That is an occupational hazard for older persons. Joe had trouble making the stairs, his legs hurt from decreasing circulation.

Joe got smart. He got out of the house and cleaned up litter from the streets and parkways in the area where he lived. Everybody says how great of Joe to do this for everyone. Joe did not volunteer, he was not hired, got no pay.

All Joe got was—busy. Once again he had a usefulness, a role in life. Perhaps, as he says, he is clean crazy, but Joe has something to get up for day after day. And his legs stopped hurting and now he takes the stairs two at a time. Joe better watch out that he doesn't trip and break an ankle or a hip or something. But he is alive—again.

Parishes can serve as idea headquarters; committees and persons can suggest, point the way, open new doors for older persons to become reinvolved.

Purpose—being useful and needed—is not an automatic condition among all older persons. Many simply resign from the human race; others retreat into their own self-fulfilling shell of loneliness. They are convinced no one needs them anymore. Feeling lonely and forgotten, and living that way, often results in their being lost. We need to find them again, and draw them back out of their aloneness. We are all lonely or bored sometimes, but staying that way is a decision, and probably a grievous sin besides, because each of us—and each and every member of the older generation as well—is needed to help brighten and lighten these retirement years of our sisters and brothers in the church.

Each older person is an individual, a person with specific attributes, interests, and concerns. We all need this experience of sharing ourselves—getting out of our own selves and back into community.

ACTION SUGGESTIONS

Never Too Late for Goal Setting

An excellent exercise: Pass around paper, pen or pencil, and ask for 15 minutes of quiet thought. Suggest they dream a bit about what "they would still like to try, and to accomplish."

What unfinished tasks in life need scheduling in their lives? which can they give higher priority to? which tasks, in which order, and what kind of timetable?

Suggest they think big, reach out, imagine the unimaginable, throw off inhibitions; remind them that they are free, and older, but for the living it is never too late.

Next Comes Group Sharing

Put four to six together around a table or in a circle; ask them to pick their group leader for this next step. Ask that they now share and discuss what each has written. Encourage open and cheerful friendliness around each table.

What you are after is openness and imagination (and why not try this or that?). You will want to have a natural commitment result from, first, the internalizing, the writing down; then when they have openly shared their goals, they will be making a commitment to themselves, and in front of others.

Finally, Write Some Goals Down Publicly

Ask for volunteer goal sharing; on a blackboard or newsprint tablet write all the best goal ideas, as many as you can. Then have group members discuss. See if any of the goals are the kind which can best be achieved by two or more persons. If so, make sure that you begin the process of nailing down who will do what with whom. What we are after here are stated and shared goals, for as many individuals as will do this; but also, you will be after getting two or more involved with each other—in an appealing activity in which they can share, which can be managed and accomplished together.

Parish ministry to the retired, the aging and alone, can be—and it is so desperately needed—a reaching out and finding; a regathering together of those "lost souls" who too often wallow sadly in their aloneness. We must organize this effort to invite and carry them back into community, back into the world of being wanted and needed and endlessly useful.

If It's Not Their Program, They Won't Own It

In all of this finding and helping the elderly in our parish midst, one word of experienced caution. Let no program become too much of a do-good activity that only makes *you*, the enabler, feel good. Let's not make aging cripples by doing this and that for them.

Find them; enlist their ideas and suggestions, find out what they need, what they may lack in their alone lives; make idea suggestions and lead them around to where the programs initiated become theirs. Determine what can be done *by* and *with* the elderly—not just *for* them.

Open doors; sprinkle ideas around; get them started and then offer to check back from time to time to see how they are doing—*for and by themselves.*

The most successful Senior Citizen Center (City of Manitowoc Multipurpose Senior Center) we have ever discovered is in Manitowoc, Wisconsin. There are over 5,000 members involved, in varying frequency. The secret of their success was simply applying the sensible approach of finding out what they needed and wanted; and then helping show them how it could be attained. This exciting group has just now moved into a brand new community-provided (through a city referendum) facility which cost near $1 million. It is *their* place and *they* decided what *they* needed; they determined how it would be managed and by whom; it is truly *theirs.*

Bernice Barta, the very practical facilitator who helped most to show these people "their own way" delights in telling that now, no one, no matter how aggressive nor how much a leader, could ever take this place over, or warp it to personal goals or ambition. She insists that this is their idea and their place, and their responsibility. Truly, this is the roadmap—albeit grander than needed by our churches—of how to succeed. Apparently, by searching out what it is they want and need; to find out how to get it, how to make it all happen; and then, ever so gently guiding those who will make it happen—by and for themselves. They own their own success. No condescending or fawning do-good generosity can provide as well as self-interest can that which the elderly of any place can and will make happen and enjoy managing for themselves.

All persons need to feel involved, to have a role they can be comfortable with and which, in large part, they have made for themselves.

What we in the church can do is recognize who the elderly are, what they can still do and how we can help enable them to create and involve themselves—with others—in their own ministry. Their retirement can be our signal that here are more missionaries, more disciples for our parish ministry for older persons. Invite, and enroll them—for their needs and for our help.

We Seldom Challenge Older Persons' Hidden Talents/Skills

Helen Trendly and Joan Bishop are amateur writers, poets. Oh, they aren't all that amateur anymore since each has been published some and each has won at least one or two awards.

Now they win awards of another kind since they are "teaching a poetry class" in an extended care nursing home. The students are for the most part older ladies and most of them had never written anything before. They learn form, and the conservation of words and how to power-pack in the emotions of daily human experiences.

There are two stars, but one shines ever so much more brightly. Eighty-four-year-old Magdalen Selberg had previously tried her hand at writing but gave it up because of family and other living pressures. Now she is newly fulfilled, and her present late-in-life poetic creations will probably "have to be" published—they are that good.

There is much more here than just poetry and old ladies writing verse. There is that discovery of sensitivity and personal and emotional expression, but there is also this new finding of latent talent and current joy and usefulness.

Our challenge, in Christian parishes, must and can be to provide a climate, a possibility, that those who are now older may find the way—and the encouragement of opportunity—to make of these later years still one more new career. And the last can be better than the first if we offer, if we provide facility and expectation, and if we show that we expect their unending usefulness in new ministries of their own. The question—and it is one we ought to challenge and direct them toward—is simply this: "What are you and I now going to do with this great and golden gift of available and uncommitted free time?" It is not for us to tell them but rather to show them the way, how their own dreams may be further fulfilled.

The Chicago Catholic Archdiocese, through its Catholic Charities organization, provides a fascinating array of services for Senior Citizens (and if it can be done in such a large and overwhelming metropolis, it should be possible anywhere). They have a publication called *Keen-Ager News*, which recounts and informs about the work and activities of the Senior Senate and of the efforts and successes of the staff and volunteers who give life and breath to whatever missions may arise or be instigated by them.

One wise way they manage both to involve the local parish persons and to conserve the time and energy of the enabling staff/volunteer persons, is to help in organizing local clubs in parishes—and in getting the new groups off the ground. The experienced support persons attend three or four meetings, enough to make sure the group is going. After that they fade away—to other needed places. They come back usually only when invited. In this way, the new group becomes its own responsibility, each in its own way.

Beyond that, this committed success group at headquarters also takes part in issue-oriented activities. They press and encourage; they inform the unaware; they help get things started—even lower-cost senior housing; they advise on citizen (seniors expecially) tax refund rights. They are activists (Ombudsman/woman) in behalf of seniors who live by themselves.

This is just one striking example of what can and is being done:

Together Is Better; Two Gathered in My Name; There Am I Also

Sally Minton is a parish lay worker. One of her successes has been the bringing together of neglected and alone persons—with another person—to form a small community with the umbrella auspices of her church. Better than family in many ways, and augmenting the particular relationship family members have, she finds that each gets a new friend, that each relates in candor and a new warmth with the other.

What Sally admires is that her new charges make a vital new acquaintance with whom they can be open; to share troubles and concerns with; someone who may be called upon in time of turmoil and trouble. Sally Minton has performed her ministry by bringing two like souls together, then she fades away and goes on to other persons and ministries. She has made two lonely and fearful persons find a new kinship, a new reason for still being a person.

Tithing with Time and Talent Counts as Well

Think of all of the alone persons—those you know and see and those of whom you have no awareness. There are over 25 million seniors past 65 now; and their number will climb to 35 million by the end of the century or sooner. Many of those are neglected persons and many have little or no contact, at least of a pleasant nature, from month to month.

Olaf Jergensen was one such alone, and very lonely, person. He lived in one room with an ordinary bed, one chair, a modest chest of drawers, and no closet. Finally, Olaf's room moved in on him and he screamed to the local F.I.S.H. organization. After many false starts, these devoted volunteers found another older guy, also a bit hard of hearing, to get to be so called buddies with. They chatted about the olden days and generally filled their empty days more fully. A simple, but vital, form of ministry anyone can help with.

This is such an evident ministry for so many of us who have our health and who have the time. But what specifically can just a few persons do to get sharing with the aging?

ACTION: FOSTERING NEW RELATIONSHIPS

- *Form small teams* which offer problem-solving help in helping make contact with the required expert.
- *Take the older person* along with you to civil and governmental offices, to Social Security and Medicare offices, in order to make certain they get helpful information they need for problem solving.
- *Make contact* with information and referral offices to help locate community services and data which the solitary elderly may not know how to secure.
- *Bring them a gift*—a bowl of soup, or just yourself. Bring something you enjoyed reading and now wish to share. Go prepared to write letters for them if that idea is indicated. Older persons generally try to avoid the appearance of being

a burden; help in small but vital human ways. Your kindness will fill many pleasant days of remembering.

- *Always be happily positive* and let these people know they still have choices, and hope, and your love.

ACTION/ACTIVITY SUGGESTIONS

From the retirement, wellness, death and dying, and the stages of grief sections in the foregoing, you and your group should be able to prepare a profile of the aged and set forth a set of goals and objectives which take these factors into account as ingredients affecting your aging ministry.

Chapter II

How to Administer a Senior Ministry

Here are some ideas for a congregation and its pastor, having decided that a ministry to, with, and by older people is desired. Remember, every group and every leader will have his/her own procedure for accomplishing the task, but there are certain common denominators that have proven successful and may be utilized in your group. Much of the following is to be considered as a "model" from which modifications and adaptations are expected. Consider the following as a guideline if you are ready to move.

1.

First, *gather a group of persons committed to establishing a ministry by the elderly.* Members of the congregation presently retired, active, and mobile may be invited to a planning meeting along with other persons younger in age. You will find the differences in ages will often be more of a help than a hindrance. The key factor is not age, but motivation. Concentrate on senior adults to run their own ministries. This is generally possible. Note from the start, this is not to be a ministry of "doing for" but rather of "doing with." The healthy philosophy of a successful senior ministry demands "ownership" of the program by the older persons. Involve the seniors from the start. Ask for their opinions, discover their needs, and share with them this exciting ministry. Determine 8 to 14 people interested in a senior ministry, and take the initiative to invite them to a planning meeting.

ACTION SUGGESTIONS/MANAGING WITHOUT NAGGING

> *Words of warning:* If it isn't their program, unless they can come to "own" it, it may not get to be much of a program; or it may drift along and eventually die.

A. Parish committee task: find the elderly, both those who have remained visible, and those who may have disappeared into aloneness.
B. Take a parish survey; enlist parochial or Sunday school children; do a superficial census of the neighborhood— block by block. Remember today we have many invisible lost souls hidden away in apartments.
C. Once you find them, make lists and try some normal

groupings for inviting, for pickup and return. Set a first planning event.

D. At the first meeting have quiz forms available; do some brainstorming (any idea is written down, not judged, not accepted or rejected). But keep these guide forms for later. Better to make all of these ideas their ideas, their suggestions. What you want is to find out what *they* want, what *they* feel they need. It may help if you spot a few natural leaders, and not the overwhelming who turn off the underaggressive. Let these leaders quietly assist in drawing some consensus together.

E. Set another date for sorting out (you and your assistants will have done some prior sorting out but not enough to spoil the group spontaneity). You will want to let their priority and timetable wishes prevail, but you will also want to make sure that the jobs get done.

F. Ask them to set next meeting dates; ask if some of these early activities might develop better if managed by subcommittees; and if so, suggest they name who will do what. It will probably help most if you and your sponsoring committee persons seem to be too busy and otherwise occupied to do much followthrough. You will of course follow through but imperceptibly. Trick is to get them to organize themselves, for what they want and need, and to offer yourself and the parish facilities, etc. Get 'em going!

2.

Second, *offer a method of determining some of the needs of the older person.* You may wish to start the discussion in the planning meeting about older people with three questions:

A. Who are the elderly?

B. What can the older person do?

C. How can the older person be enabled to perform?

Through this method seniors will feel they have been called together for a purpose which will soon be obvious: the needs and desires of senior people. Give an unmistakable impression that you want the older people to tell you what they want and what they need. In the process, there may be some valid discoveries. Studies indicate that clergy are not always correct in acknowledging, evaluating or enunciating the needs of older people.[1]

Following that good beginning, you will want to determine some specific facts. Some of the facts will include the number of retirees or people over 65 in congregational membership. There might be some consideration given to the number of senior citizens in the immediate neighborhood of the church. That is how the Good Shepherd program in Kansas City originated.[2] They concluded their church facilities could offer services and be utilized to meet some of the needs of the older people. Two major concerns older persons face are *loneliness* and *loss of purpose.* Considering these two basic needs common to all older people, your congregation may utilize its facilities to permit some resolutions, to meet some of these common needs.

Not all congregations have—or should be expected to have—the resources to serve all the concerns of their elderly members.

ACTION SUGGESTIONS/LISTING LOCAL AREA RESOURCES

Governmental Agencies Available:

A. Each state has a State Commission on Aging with countless available services, professionals and information which can be of great help to anyone in that particular state.

B. States are also divided into Area Agencies on Aging, and through this grouping of a number of counties, many excellent and dedicated professionals can be inestimably helpful.

C. Many counties have a County Commission on Aging, and these are very helpful in handling discount programs (qualifying cards), nutrition programs, and many others. Call upon them.

D. In many communities there are Senior Citizen Centers, Golden Age Homes, and other such organizations and facilities. Check around and tie in all you can with existing programs and staffs.

Many clergy and church leaders are ignorant of available services and aids for senior citizens. (Information regarding available services is included in the bibliographical data of this manual.) One pastor of one congregation located in a high-density senior citizen area was simply amazed to discover the help that was available, informational presentations for the asking, and assistance in resolving some of the physical needs his members experienced. Everyone engaged in this senior ministry should feel compelled to investigate the Area Agency for Aging office, the Community Service office, or whatever office for the aging operates in that community. Beyond the actual physical, sociological and psychological help available to older people, agencies offer films, visual aids, printed literature, and personal advice. The field is literally unlimited. It simply takes a beginning.

ACTION SUGGESTIONS/RESOLVING SOME OF THE NEEDS

How Seniors Can Meet Some New Obligations

A. *Make list of persons*, and types of persons, who might have need for me, for what I can bring in love, in sharing, in my presence:

_____

_____

B. *List personal health* and welfare habits and practices I can and will now change to make me safer for these rewarding later years:

_____

_____

C. Decision to *expand my circle* of active relationships to include with a personal visit, such as:
   1. an alone person
   2. a younger person
   3. a handicapped, shut-in, or hospitalized person

_____

_____

D. Find a few ways in which my particular *skills and experience* can be of specific help to persons (specify what kinds of persons) who could benefit from my sharing of these:

_____

_____

Please consider the above as something to think about. Parish committee for seniors should be urged to add and alter according to specific situations.

3.

God Opens Doors for You

You will soon discover some *senior centers* in your area. These centers offer a variety of services and programs. The services offered in one center in South Florida include physical care, psychological counseling, recreational activity, educational discoveries, and other life satisfactions for the elderly. One pastor, while searching for help for one of his senior members, soon discovered nominal cost meals were available within walking distance. The near starvation condition of his member was changed, and almost immediately the older person exhibited a change in life-style. Following the meal, the older member found enjoyment in socializing with some of his neighbors and soon after participated in a craft offered at the senior center. This older person had experienced what gerontologists call "self-actualization." Social interaction is very important in the lives of older people. Older people tend to isolate themselves. Nutrition centers and service centers serve as a natural gathering place. Socialization immediately resolves many other needs, and the degree of self-satisfaction is increased.

Needs of the elderly, however, are not always resolved. The reason is not so much lack of information as the inability of the older person to use the service available. A senior citizen responded to the community visitor, "I have no way of getting there." Once transportation was arranged, the older person began enjoying companionship, enrolled in at least one educational course, and now regularly enjoys a noon meal at the neighborhood senior service center.

Smiling Might Postpone Your Wheelchair Time

Bertha pushes wheelchairs at a large nursing home; no one hired her and she did not even volunteer. After coming to this nursing home for three or more years to visit older relatives who have since gone on to their heavenly home, Bertha just kept returning.

Noticing that quite a number of patients never ever had a visitor, she decided to begin to be one. She pushes patients in their wheelchairs, to the dining areas, to therapy, to chapel or the TV room.

And Bertha smiles broadly all the while. It finally became apparent why she had such an open and loving smile: Bertha was aware, and happily grateful, that she was not yet living in one of those wheelchairs herself.

"I complained about my shoes until I met a man who had no feet."

The agenda for your initial meeting should include listing and investigation of services offered by the local community, but be ready to facilitate the services which are available. You will immediately experience responses of thanks, and indebtedness from the older persons and members of their respective families.

Sharing Potluck—Automatic Community for Older Persons

Four lively, eighty-plus ladies report they never eat Sunday dinner alone anymore. They always go out to eat together, mostly to new and different places. Since none of them drives anymore, someone takes them or they call a cab.

During the week they are most apt to operate in pairs, endlessly switching the "who's coming to my house this time" routine. They bring portable ingredients with the hostess normally fixing the meat or other hot dish. Not all are banquet meals since, as they say, they are older ladies now and don't need all that much to eat anymore. But they have happy attitudes and enjoy being together, whether on Sunday with all four or on weekday evenings when there may be just two of them.

What they are demonstrating at their advanced age is that it is usually not necessary to be alone too much of the time, unless one wishes to have private time.

Leadership Clues

You may want to include a questionnaire in your search to discover ways of serving and bringing about resolutions for specific needs. In the appendixes of this manual you will find some sample questionnaires which may prove helpful. Provide opportunity for those attending your meetings to contribute their wisdom and expertise. Obtain their suggestions and recommendations. On a chalkboard make a list of the needs of the aging, potentials, interests, and talents. List the three greatest concerns of the group. Ask, what are the alternatives? Try using the form below and fill in the three greatest needs, potentials, interests, and talents of your group.

Needs	Potentials	Interests	Talents
1. _____	1. _____	1. _____	1. _____
2. _____	2. _____	2. _____	2. _____
3. _____	3. _____	3. _____	3. _____
4. _____	4. _____	4. _____	4. _____

You will want to consider some future plans for your senior ministry. You will be looking for group aims and goals, and specific tasks and tactics necessary to implement some of your objectives. Be sure to establish target dates for each task and determine a responsible individual from the group to lead or carry out the task. (There is a form for your convenience in the appendixes.) The underlying key to success is to be specific and pertinent. Don't settle for generalities. Name the needs, specify the problems, and spell out your ideas for resolutions.

If you are interested in organizing a leadership group, you may wish to elect a temporary chairman. In one case, a group of four people were selected, at the suggestion of both the group and the pastor, to serve as leaders and to present programs and projects for the entire group. The smaller group exchanged some ideas concerning the purpose, and went to work immediately planning programs, setting dates, and assigning duties to accomplish their plans. The group succeeded. There was daily contact by telephone with one another, and by the time the events were to take place, everyone knew what the other person was responsible for. The program succeeded. What happened was, subgroups were assigned, and they in turn communicated with one another. The leaders considered who would do what to accomplish the goal. Participants may divide into subcommittees for specific functions and may undertake appropriate research for actions through personal interviews, field studies, questionnaires, and many other kinds of data gathering. Be sure that each individual is familiar with what he or she is to do, has the ability to accomplish the task, and is willing to meet deadlines.

Iowa Church Had Elderly Listen to How It Is for Others

Out in Council Bluffs one pastor got his older people together for a simple cake and coffee meeting. The program he had set up was also most simple.

Pastor Schuh had asked four newly retired couples to come to meet with some others of the congregation and to share how it is when workers get retired and come home to stay. They explained how two people in the same house full time, and underfoot, can get to be a problem. Their suggestions included that the man of the house should get out of the house; that he should have outside activity so the wife who is not at all retired from her homemaker job would still have her independence.

Many of Pastor Schuh's spokespersons had a lot of good things to share about retirement and its blessings. Best of all, they liked the freedom to do what they wished, to go where they decided, and to invest their days in what pleased them. Most of the ladies present also had a great deal to tell about what retirement can do to the lady of the house unless things get sensibly worked out early.

Helping Wives Cope with Widowhood

Ruth Squires is not unlike so many other wives who lose their husbands and then get lost themselves. As part of the grief process they say they want to be alone—to work it all out. For some this may be good and necessary, but others need ventilating opportunities for their confusion.

After family and friends had departed, Ruth noticed that she was indeed going to be quite alone from now on, unless she herself took steps to get involved.

She made a long list of those things which she now feared most to be doing alone for the first time. And one by one, Ruth braced herself and went out and did these tough things such as actually being seen eating out with a man (most of those were professionals she needed to consult with, men who had been close to her husband and who now were anxious to help). Having done them once, this simple exercise gave her the strength to do these and other tasks again, and again.

Father Higginbottom Gets Older Persons Growing Gardens

Most of us who are past 50 had some childhood home garden experience. Perhaps it was more work than fun when we were kids and busy at hoeing, weeding, and digging. But now, all of that can be fun. Besides, at today's prices, we can save a lot of money.

Father Higgie, as he is affectionately known, got some near-town farmland and found a farmer willing to plow it and to till and seed long rows of the most popular and useful garden plants. Father Higgie rents the plots to parish neighbors at about $15.00 per summer.

Everybody wins. The land found excellent use; the parish families got back to the earth and enjoyed weeding, watering, and actually picking fresh and tasty vegetables once again. And the good padre has a fresh new attitude in his parish community. As with so many of these efforts, the rewards are unexpected and unbelievable.

Success is directly related to adequate leadership and training opportunities for your leaders and interested people. Following your initial action, it is very likely a volunteer force will emerge. This can be considered a "determined" ministry—one that is determined to minister to a specific group.

From now on the key is EVALUATION! Periodically evaluate your progress. Set a date for your next meeting. Consider the findings of the various committees or individuals. As a result, your ministry will begin to take form.

Special Church Services Can Help Bridge the Generation Gap

Father Murphy decided to hold a special marriage vow renewal service on Holy Family Day. After a homily that day, he asked couples to rise and to come forward according to the longevity of their marriage. First up was a couple married 60 years; then others of 50 plus, and a few golden oldsters; and on down through the forties and thirties.

Two by two, as if to the ark, they paraded happily toward the chancel along with the rest from their vintage. Their number increased as the 10- and five-year couples came forward; and in the end, there was even one 1-year couple.

Then all joined Father Murphy as they repeated after him the renewal of their marriage vows. The service impressed all the participants with the unity that binds the members of God's family over a wide span of years.

An intensive inspirational meeting of all ages, minds, and hearts will demonstrate a holistic concern of God's people for God's people. Mutual Christian concern is one of the most needed virtures of the Christian faith. Jesus Christ ministered to the whole person. The physical, emotional, psychological, mental, economical, as well as the spiritual needs of people deserve serious and sincere attention. The whole person is the total concern for God.

Prayer Partner Idea Creates Involving Community

An expanding success in Rev. Markham's congregation is the prayer partner service he and his liturgy committee introduced at Pentecost a few years ago.

Each attending parishioner writes his or her name on a slip of paper, and these are collected the Sunday prior to Pentecost. On Pentecost Sunday, each attendee draws out a slip with a name. Usually there is a phone number so the new partner might call to inquire about particular petitions or prayer needs.

As the years have gone on, each participant has a litany of new persons with whom he or she feels a special relationship. Prayer partners are a very mixed universe; they match an older person to a child, or like to like, or a church member with the pastor. Not only is a specific purpose served thereby, but there is also a spreading creation of concern in a community of loving souls.

A single tall-stemmed rose appeared at our house one day for my wife. The card read simply: "From your prayer partner."

You might want to run through the following checklist as a help in formulating *the role and function of the committee* assuming the leadership of your group. The following questions may be used by you and shared with your leaders, or you may want to utilize them as part of the agenda for your congregational ministry.

1. What group of persons does this activity deal with?
2. Are the people served involved in decisionmaking?
3. What does the activity seek to accomplish?
4. Does the activity get at the underlying issue or only symptoms?
5. Does it meet valid needs?
6. Does it address future needs?
7. Is the group capable of implementing the activity?
8. What effect will the activity have on the greater community?
9. Will the activity produce a model that can be copied?
10. Is there assurance of continued future support of the activity?
11. Is the budget realistic?
12. Does the activity have some evaluation process?
13. Does the activity have to be "successful" to be effective?
14. Does the activity duplicate efforts?
15. Is there something for which the congregation can be known?

These are suggestions. They may well lead to decisions, conclusions, or exciting new beginnings. Use them for your good. Share them with those involved. Review them after you have started.

Parishes can bring in resource persons to talk turkey. For example: The aging worry about not having enough income, enough health insurance to overlap with Medicare's inadequacy. They sit on top of appreciating homes and other property—but they are reported to be living on dog food because they "can't afford" to eat properly.

First off, that's nonsense. Even the poor, and especially they, can get supplemental security income; they can qualify for Medicaid, food stamps, and other benefits.

But the rest of us should hear from knowledgable experts about what our true net worth really means; how it can help be a support for our later needs. Certified public accountants, articulate bankers, and some lawyers might be happy to stop by for an hour's dialog—to lighten the worry load of some older persons.

There is a kind of fairplay justice which requires that we understand and acknowledge just how (relatively) well off most of us really are, so that we stop living poor (at least poor in spirit) before we end up dying rich without ever noticing that we always had choices and chances for sharing.

Surrogate Children and Grandchildren: Parish Power at Work

With the nuclear family of today, older persons live on one coast while the kids live on the other. Or the aging go off to warmer retirement communities while the young families remain back home. In all of this there is a breakdown in activity and daily sharing of loving relationships. The telephone is great but it cannot replace seeing, hearing in person, face-to-face meeting and touching.

And the loving young of our families do miss their parents and grandparents as much as they are also missed.

Effective parish projects and programs for older persons can help to harness them to younger people, and in this way each generation benefits. And, there can be bonuses when preschool children are brought along and there is still one more generation for sharing with grandparents. Harness the surrogates and spread good cheer in both directions.

Encourage Oldsters to Internalize Not Generalize

Parish liturgies can do so much for individuals if they filter from theology down to where life is experienced. For example: instead of just having the usual crib or Christmas tree at or near the sanctuary, one parish committee has come up with a novel idea.

The tree begins to fill with stars (silver, gold, and white paper stars) from the first Sunday in Advent until Christmas Day. On these stars individual members are urged to note a special petition, or special thanksgiving message, and this then is hung on the church community tree until it grows and fills with both petitions and stars of thanksgiving.

Best of all, persons have been motivated to internalize, to think and to relate to their heavenly Father, to appeal to His loving care and to say their needs and gratitude. And they do this, not only quietly as private individuals but also as members of their church community.

Ingredients for Getting Started

Here are some recommendations. Again use them at your own discretion. They do work. They are also to be considered as guidelines rather than rules. Alter and adopt at will.

1. *Commit yourself to begin.* You do not have to start with elaborate programs, but you do need to get under way. One member tosses a rock into a pond. Soon the ripple is moving other areas, and soon after the circle becomes bigger and bigger.

2. *Get going with those who want to get going.* A few people are enough to begin with. It is better to have a few and learn, than to have many and flounder and even fail. Many ministries with older persons have begun with the meeting of a dozen people or less. Ideas were shared, decisions were made, and experience became the best teacher.

3. *Be selective in choosing programs and services.* Keep this question before you: "What do the people need most, now?" Find out by asking. Using questionnaires, have key people observe and stay alert, interview constantly, and by all means observe needs personally.

4. *Package deeds meeting needs in an attractive, winsome way.* The ministry must be exciting, inspiring, and joyous. This ministry is new. Very few churches are involved seriously in a specific ministry dealing with needs of older people. Leaders must be sincere and effective. Members of the groups will respond to their peers and leaders. You will find this part of the ministry most rewarding.

5. Whatever is done, *make it a quality program.* It is discouraging and debilitating to have a first-class idea executed in a fourth-class manner. A quality program can be accomplished by properly training, appropriately leading, and encouraging those who do their jobs well.

6. *Finally, grow from here.* The batter has to hit the ball before he can run to first base. Others will have to hit it before he can move to second,

or to third base. Before you is the challenge to get the bat off your shoulder and hit the ball. In terms of middle age and older persons ministries, you may already be on first or second base and now you want to get home. To accomplish that goal you will need ideas and leadership. Keep searching. Try new methods again and again. Enjoy the ministry that unfolds before you. Nothing is holding you back besides yourself. The rewards are beyond measure.

Carrying Out the Program

1. Know interests, needs and resources through research and surveys

4. Evaluate program at regular intervals

2. Determine priorities, plan appropriate programs or action

 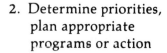

3. Find facilities, persons, materials, funding

Let's Say a Good Word About Senility

Ninety-five percent of us are never going to become senile. So why worry so much about losing our minds when we hit the really later years?

It may also be true that a lot of us have plenty that we ought to be forgetting anyway—human things like hurts, slights, envy, and the like. Most of us, as we grow older, do a better job of remembering the olden days than we do of remembering yesterday. There is a comfort in that too, since those good old olden days in most cases take on a better shine than they had while we were living them.

Senility in its varying degrees must actually be one of God's last gifts to the truly elderly. The nicest thing we of parishes can do is understand that and not bring sadness when we go to visit those who have lost either total or intermittent contact with reality. Some of them drift in and then phase out, but our visits can still serve great good as they add an awareness of our love and concern to the lucid times. Let's build in some special visits with the unremembering; it can be a good lesson to the visitors.

Taking Short Trips into Nature's Open University

Easy to manage anywhere are short junkets of older persons who go off together, by bus, by a group of cars, to visit zoos, arboretums, flower gardens, and the like. Often, it is enough to go in search of and study mushrooms; or spring wildflowers, or of autumn nutting times. It's fun, it is outdoors, it vastly improves interest in natural things, it opens new avenues of more intent observation.

Awareness of the world around us, with reawakening

interest, with newly acquired knowledge, these are life enrichments at their best. Both men and women can play in this game. It usually costs little or nothing. Sometimes knowledgable professionals can help share their data, they might show experiments in process, there may be films, so many ways in which nature's doors can be reopened to the aging.

Try a Little Heritage Rejuvenation to Interest the Elderly

People are scrambling into the "roots business." They want to dig back into where they came from, where their ancestors came from, what kind of folks they were. All of this gives them a perspective on who they really are.

There are a lot of facilities, and there are a lot of helpful experts. Get some of these persons into the parish events, and let them light this fire of interest in some of your older persons. Easy to get into—but not easy to finish—research of this ancestry business. But think what it can mean to aging persons to start all over to remember and check out and share data about which European country, which old world parish, which American Indian tribe, or wherever they had their beginnings.

What is really involved here is the reestablishment of real persons. Pride of this kind is constructive, it is not un-Christian; it makes life fascinating—and gets people so busy and interested they won't have time to fret about much else.

Case History of a Senior Ministry

One congregation called a meeting to establish a senior ministry. Telephone calls were made, and at the first meeting fifteen senior members of the congregation attended. Soon leaders were appointed, both by the group and by encouragement from the pastor. The leaders directed their attention to the growing number of older people in this particular congregation. A study was made regarding:

- The fastest-growing portion of the population;
- The current percentage of senior citizens in membership with this particular parish;
- The total lack of attention relative to organization concerned with older people offered by this congregation

It was not very long before weekly meetings were arranged, but they proved to be too frequent for those participating in this new ministry. Bimonthly meetings were soon scheduled, projects and programs were presented, and a group of no less than 30 or more persons participated on a regular basis the first year.

Their Findings:

Several theoretical or functional aspects began to emerge. Three specific needs were discovered:
    A. The group needed *SOCIALIZATION.* The constant call was heard for tours and trips, games and togetherness. It appeared very

significant to the leaders of this group that card games, or activities which divided the group were not as well received as joint activities such as bingo or a bus tour.

B. The group needed *EDUCATIONAL INFORMATION.* These seniors were happy to learn about physical aids and sources of help, but avidly avoided identifying themselves with physical impairment. Gerontologists have made it clear this is to be anticipated. The older person recognizes the imminence of death, for example, but will do all in his or her power to avoid personal identification with the suffering or the disabled. On the other hand, the group welcomed life-support information. Nutrition courses and related presentations were to come. The older persons proved themselves to be like other age groups interested in life and living rather than death and dying.

C. *INSPIRATION* was a third element introduced to this group of seniors. The pastor was the usual leader in any of the formal presentations. Prayer times were spent praying for some child or family member in special need. There were Bible crossword puzzles. There were more serious or formal presentations, often discussing doctrines or practices of the church. Inspiration and spiritual growth is one of the basic needs in senior ministry. This may come as a surprise, but older people need counseling, assurance, as well as consolation. Older people can learn, memorize, even though they gently protest, "Those days are gone forever."

HOW TO GET STARTED SUMMARY—Check the following:

1. Have you a group of persons committed to start a ministry?
2. What are some of the needs of older persons?
3. Are you familiar with community resources?
4. Have you organized to organize?
5. Who will be your leaders?
6. Are you evaluating your programs?
7. Have you considered a new and different approach?
8. How are you answering the need for socialization, education, and inspiration?

ACTION/ACTIVITY SUGGESTIONS

To Reinvolve and Remotivate Older Persons in Parishes

1. By any census method, be it cursory or thorough (to begin with), find the older persons in your parish. Do this as part of other census gathering within the parish or as a specific exercise. Census data has many uses.
2. Gather a representative parish committee, and have each member list all known persons, or likely locations, and melt these into a beginning census; ask selected persons to call in person or by phone to complete census data of the elderly and retired.

3. Announce a special combination spiritual and social event for older persons in the near future.
4. Firm up a committee of interested parish members, including surrogate sons and daughters, and with them set up your plan for finding, remotivating, and reinvolving your older persons. Hold event for elderly.
5. Have basic plans—at least a skeleton for action; for getting started together—but make it clear from the beginning that this is to be "their" program, that they can plan and do whatever they wish.
6. Offer support, supervisory checking-in, but suggest they get organized with a beginning list of events, with start-up scheduling, and with volunteer or assigned leaders from their midst—to get the ball rolling.
7. To begin with, it helps to have handout suggestions from which they may wish to choose or to which they may prefer to add their own ideas, suggestions, and wishes.
8. Repeat your offer of facilities they may use for getting started; and for meeting later on. Assure them of your parish's interest and concern, but insist that this is to be *their own program;* except that you and the select committee persons stand willing to meet again with them at later times—to rekindle any lapsed enthusiasms, to suggest new and added ways to reach out further in this fresh new parish ministry by and with the older persons, for themselves, and for their fellowmen.

Chapter III

Socialization Needs and Opportunities

"Gemuetlichkeit" is the German term for good times, fellowship, cheer, and good will. The term may be German, but it is a common concern for those considering ministering to, with, for, and by older people. An English equivalent of the German word for our purpose is socialization.

A ministry with socialization can be the foundation for an exciting array of purposeful services and projects. The Southern Baptist Convention approached the problem of a ministry of the aging by declaring, "A mere cycle of games, trips, entertainment, and handcrafts wears thin. Helping others to play games, taking others on trips, entertaining others, and making handcrafts for others, these activities give the dimension and provide the setting for the discovery of meaning."

Various ministries should be considered. If your efforts are directed toward services, fellowship, or whatever, develop that purpose and more likely than not you will have answered the need of the moment.

As an idea bank, some of the following suggestions will not be feasible or useful for you. However, there may be a new idea, something you had not thought about, and just that spark for your ministry may be worth consideration.[1]

A. *Telephone Reassurance.* To some this may seem too simple, too impersonal, or unproductive. The beauty of the program is its simplicity, the fact that some days it is the only personal contact for the receiver, and the accumulation of small efforts by someone else which enriches lives. A good way to start a telephone reassurance ministry is to:

1. *Recruit a coordinator.* He or she will listen to problems and try to be a troubleshooter. His or her main responsibility will be to coordinate the entire ministry.
2. *Recruit a support committee.* Volunteers will be needed. This is never a one-person ministry. Too much time and effort are needed for a single individual to accomplish the task.
3. *Allocate some funds.* There will be some postage and other survey and printing needs. Records need to be kept, and this all costs money.
4. *Keep records.* A full file on callers and listeners with all pertinent information will be necessary. Discovering some true needs will be assessed from these records.
5. *Recruit volunteers.* Training is needed regarding some do's and don'ts.
6. Evaluate the program periodically. It might be well to have a monthly meeting of the group involved in this ministry to check up on the program.

Some telephone reassurance ministries are conducted during the morning hours. Other telephones have been used in the evening. The time and length of conversations seem to be determined by the callers and the receivers.

Here are some helpful pointers regarding this ministry:

1. Make it very clear to everyone this service will be discontinued if the listener fails to inform the caller that he or she will not be able to answer the phone at the appointed time.

2. The listener should sign a legal release exempting the telephone reassurance ministry and its sponsors from responsibility for medical costs or property damage resulting from forced entry during an emergency.

3. Telephone companies in some areas have special low charges for low-income residents, provide volume control amplifiers for modest fees, and offer other services for the elderly and the disabled.

This ministry is known by various names, such as, Care-Ring, Telecheck, Telecare, TLC (Telephone Line to the Community), and STEP (Services to Elderly Persons).

Information on training techniques, cost, evaluation procedures, and listing of resource centers across the nation is available from the National Council on the Aging (NCOA), 1828 L. Street, N.W., Washington, DC 20036; ask for "SOS-14": Establishing Telephone Reassurance Services by Sandra K. Match.

Living Too Alone Can be Bad for Their Health

Two retired school teachers were discovered by their parish team to have been living well below the poverty and sensible health care level society owes older persons. But they were not discovered—and might never have been if one had not fallen and broken her hip.

Concerned about big city security problems and the difficulty of shopping and carrying their groceries up three flights of stairs at their apartment building, they had taken to staying in and living on what they had—on crackers mostly. No one knew that these educated and formerly involved persons were having any problem at all. ·

If it hadn't been for the broken hip which forced them to rise to the surface of community awareness, they might both have died of malnutrition. Apparently a daily diet of nothing but crackers and water is not adequate to maintain a balanced health condition. There was, in this case, no problem about money to provide enough food, but that did not prevent an almost fatal—and sadly unnecessary—accident. It is pleasant to report that the hospital suitably renourished both ladies and they are now living a livelier new life-style.

B. *Anyone Can Play the Monitoring Game.* Lots of enlightened older persons refuse to wallow in loneliness. They solve their separateness in creative ways. One ladies' twosome has a coffeebreak by telephone since neither finds it easy to be with the other in person. But they do not deplore their loss. They have fun having a coffeebreak by telephone.

Another, perhaps more worldly, duo who are unable to be out much anymore have their social chat of the day with a sherry break at five in the afternoon—again by telephone. Main thing is having a friend to chat with.

Many, many seniors, especially those all alone or housebound, have systems arranged with neighbors whereby shades must be raised by 10 a.m. or someone will get a checkup phone call. Others do their monitoring by telephone. In all such cases we are witnessing the creative possibilities for recreating community, even where it may not be easy. What counts is making the possible happen.

C. *How About Transportation?* This may be the easiest ministry to establish or the most difficult. Personal and private transportation may at times be arranged among the older people themselves. This, of course, would be the easiest and perhaps most effective. Beside offering the needed transportation, there are other benefits, including fellowship, service to one another, and natural concerns for the wellbeing of someone else. But there are also difficulties. The matter of insurance: should an accident occur, and personal injury is sustained, who is responsible? Private and personal transportation does have its hazards at times. Supplementary service is another possibility. Public transportation may be arranged, such as Social Security transportation vehicles. And then there is the taxi, which is expensive, but a means to an end.

D. *Trips and Tours.* This is another opportunity for senior fellowship and should be considered a major means of reaching, touching, and enriching the lives of the older persons. However, trips must be planned carefully. Consider the following (obvious) checklist a necessity for successful touring:
    1. Decide where to go.
    2. How will you get there?
    3. How long will it take?
Once you have arrived at your destination, check:
    1. What time will you return?
    2. How long will it take to load?
    3. How long will it take to return?
And don't forget:
    1. Cost per person.
    2. Publicity.
    3. Details (See pp. 41, for list of things to note in planning bus tours.)

Five Simple Remotivation Success Steps:

Lots of older persons give up; they stop trying or caring and end up unnecessarily alone and lonely. Some of this is understandable, however pointless it may seem to be. We can help:

Marion Jackson, a terminal cancer case, and a rare beauty, recited these for me from her last hospital bed. She had been asked to reinvolve and remotivate the elderly in a Wisconsin Episcopal home for older members. She sketched these steps with great effort but with a loving sharing:

1. Get the folks together, and greet each one carefully by his or her name—making a point to make the "name awareness" very singular and personal.
2. Comment about the day and say something about this place—telling for example how it reminds you of a fun day or other memorable experience you cherish. Draw out carefully from them their own memories of such a day or such a place.
3. Speak attentively and personally with each one about some interest of yours or theirs (try to have file card reminders about each member's key interests). Mention with joy about a bird you recently watched or heard; a sunset or perhaps a zoo or seaside visit; tell about a specific memory-stirring event of interest you are happy to share. This will encourage them to share from their own memory or recent experiences.
4. Speak with each person, as much as you can and always by name about recent trips, about happy experiences, a painting viewed or a book enjoyed. Store this up, make later note so that you can pick up this bridge to shared memories the next time "we all are together."
5. Once again, upon their leaving, take special pains to see and greet each one warmly and personally and mention how much you have enjoyed their shared pleasures; and be sure to make a particular point about looking forward to "our next happy visit." Build up their expectation.

E. *Socialization Without Meals, Lunches, Goodies?*
When one group was asked, "What do you do best?" almost everyone replied without hesitation: "Eat!" And eat they did. One group enjoys coffee as soon as they enter the social room of the church. Then there follows some conversation and with it a piece of coffee cake or a cookie. The noon meal or lunch finds no slackers. Socialization, eating with someone, conversation replacing the lonely apartment enjoying a new recipe—all is experienced at the table.

One group enjoyed an occasional potluck, as well as the old familiar "brown bag" lunch. This particular group found by experience that when a dish of cold cuts was ordered and the money collected, they always ended up with a profit. It became a private joke among them, "Let's have a cold-cut plate next meeting; we need the money."

F. *A Craft Ministry May Work for You.* It is the usual part of a church club, or a senior center program. If your congregation can see itself serving a broad group of the community, offering various courses, programs, enrichment enterprises, crafts in every shape and form, "models" are available everywhere. On the east coast of Florida, a university professor sparked an adult community program in which over 900 people are presently involved during the week enjoying everything imaginable, craft, education, and recreational courses. The trick is to discover what the older people of your congregation want to do. One congregation has absolutely no craft ministry, but is highly successful in its ministry to, with, for, and by older people. Since crafts were offered at every park, school, and community where these seniors resided, they discovered the seniors were in need of socialization, but not crafts. Socialization in this case was achieved by tours, trips, and games rather than handcrafts.

One of the finest models for the craft ministry is the Shepherd program located in Kansas City, Missouri. Beginning with a variety of craft and handwork books available from your local library, such a program can be launched by first making sure the following requirements are met:

1. Basic equipment
2. Methods of handling supplies
3. Organizing supplies
4. Financing craft projects
5. Inexpensive and accessible craft materials

You can use old eyeglass lenses, Christmas cards, computer cards, potato chip pails, and endless plastic bottles to make very attractive items.

In summary, as well as a review and starting point for further thought on socialization, your group should pay attention to the following considerations:

1. Provide programs.
2. Present activities.
3. Encourage handwork.
4. Programs can be both formal and informal.
5. Games will activate the group.
6. Table games versus strenuous games.
7. Bingo is always popular.
8. Cards are not enjoyed by everyone.
9. Service programs for another person.
10. Self-pleasing activities.

Many older-person ministries sponsor many of the following special ministries which you may want to consider:

1. Listening
2. Education
3. Telephone
4. Senior Center
5. Drop-in Center
6. Transportation
7. Trips and Tours
8. Prayer Groups
9. Visitation
10. Tape Ministry
11. Nutrition
12. Home Services
13. Crime Watch-Security
14. Legal Services
15. Referral and Resources
16. Crafts
17. Entertainment
18. Advocacy
19. Retreats
20. Social

Stewardship of Self

Each and every person is a unique collection of skills, interests, talents, special knowledge, and insights. We are, each one of us, often unaware that we are a bundle of resources. Sadly, and too often, we hold these worthwhile values to our secret and too-private selves—and then we end up taking them along—unused and unshared—to our ultimate resting place.

Each older person has these unappreciated depths, and they should be encouraged to tell or demonstrate what it is they may be singularly aware of; to share such ideas, knowledge, and special skills with others like themselves. These others in turn may then respond—or can be drawn out to do so—to share in return from their own storehouse of uniqueness.

All of us, and our senior friends as well, can help enrich others' lives from our own abundance of singular values and insights. In the process we gain favorable notice and support for our shy egos, and we will have lost nothing of ourselves. Actually, the sharing person enriches his own self-worth in the process of opening up to others.

ACTION/ACTIVITY SUGGESTIONS

As a fun exercise, first among your early select committee persons and later with a larger group of the older persons themselves, have each attendee jot down very informally the five first things which come into each individual's head—those talents, skills, values, interests . . . anything else . . . which are at the top of each person's self-awareness list.

This may take just a touch of prodding in some cases, but you will be delighted with all that the elderly still feel makes them singular—and it quickly builds up a "self-stewardship" inventory that can be harnessed for mutual enrichment.

Chapter IV

Education and Older Persons

Probably the most forgotten and unresearched area of senior ministry is education. Dr. William Ewers, assistant clinical professor of medicine at Vanderbilt University Medical School, said, "A person's mind need not deteriorate simply because his body ages. Many of the troubles of senility can be delayed or prevented if persons refuse to retire mentally, even if they have to retire from their jobs or cut down their activities. In essence, those who wish to keep mentally alert and healthy must stay active mentally."[1] One senior was heard to say, "I have to keep learning all my life in order to keep up with the world, otherwise I'll become dull and bored."

Propose *various kinds of educational experiences* to expand horizons of understanding for a larger percentage of your older members. This will increase their self-confidence and their potential for mutual ministry.

A. Ohio State University (among many others) offers "Program 65," in which older people in the community can register for most classes at no cost. The only condition is the availability of class space. Whenever similar opportunities are extended to the elderly, the response is impressive. This notable development in education indicates the beginning of an understanding that "there should be a social climate in this country that makes it possible for the elderly who can and wish to do so to study, grow, and enjoy themselves." College courses are being offered for credit for older persons. Around the country, older people are being invited, urged, to attend and gain some training. The results are beginning to appear. (For example: The ELDER-HOSTEL program; see listing; Selected Resources.)

B. Another package for an educational presentation is an effort by the Chicago Area AARP (American Association for Retired Persons), Chapter 2,000. The Globe Trotters presented free travel slide shows entitled: The Land of Christ's Birth, All Around South America, Hawaiian Paradise, Roads Through the Holy Land, Living in Cambodia, Yellowstone, Grand Teton, and Canadian Wonders and Alaskan Splendors.

C. Still another effort was the Retirement Expo sponsored by a church and including workshops offering information and programs relating to housing, health, nutrition, and legal services.

D. Another instruction and information vehicle is the printed newsletter. A paper may convey both congregational and community happenings, services, and benificial up-to-date facts regarding many areas of concern and interest.

In Florida, a monthly newsletter, *The Senior Consumer*, first of its kind, is available to older people. Just the mention of the newsletter and the suggestion to consider an item is enough to stir the interest and conversation of the seniors.

The Senior Consumer had an article about Condo Legislation being mired in Congress. The same issue offered the following information: "There seems to be some 'static' about hearing aids. I would be glad to offer assistance, having been in the business for the past 27 years, with 24 in Tallahassee." Another feature dealt with "Quackery: A Threat to Your Health" and still another article, "Answer to Retirement Boredom." *The Senior Consumer* is read widely by the older people in Florida and will be imitated and initiated in three Northern States this year.

E. Consider senior citizen *book centers*. The book center should include Bible studies, book reviews, a lending library bursting with information and education on many subjects, and a springboard for discussion by senior groups. Discussion groups may consider the use of Lyman Coleman's "Serendipity" books for a six- or eight-week series.

F. An individual congregation might *volunteer its facility* as a site for an American Association for Retired Persons (AARP) Chapter. This is a national organization having local chapters in many cities. The meeting consists, in part, of educational programs. Another aspect of this organization is a Defensive Driver course via films and lectures for those over 55 years of age. In a number of cities AARP also sponsors Institutes of Lifetime Learning courses, which can be conducted in the facilities of almost any church. Eight-week courses are usually held one or two hours per week on: World Affairs, Famous People of the Bible, Everyday Law, Bridge Playing, Photography, Income Tax, etc. The Cost of Crime was offered by AARP at one senior group meeting. The statistics were 30 crimes for every 1,000 persons in the general population. (This course was held in south Florida where the density of the older person leads the nation.) The facts are, say the statisticians, "older people stay in the house more, they don't get involved in arguments, they don't go out alone. It is because of fear, and it just so happens in this case, fear is functional." Continuing, the instructor warned, "the other things we must watch out for is the elderly recluse, the person who does not go out, who hides inside an apartment." These facts and figures can prove very important and helpful to older persons.

G. "The world is a great book" said St. Augustine, "of which they who never stir from the home read only a page." Many see the rest of the pages vicariously through illustrated *slide shows* given by those who have gone places and seen things. A monthly show, whether in connection with a luncheon AARP meeting, or other functions may be considered. The local library very likely has a film library, including references, description of films, and various categories for consideration. Many utility companies, large businesses, or community groups have films or visual aids available.

H. For those who travel, *a monthly bus trip* to another learning adventure may be welcome. Particular attention to details, however, is a prerequisite.

1. Arthritis may cause some seniors to think twice about boarding a high-stepped bus. Therefore, an extra step or stool should be provided.
2. Length of the tour should be considered. Older people tire more quickly than their younger counterparts.
3. Remember bathroom needs, rest stops, if a longer tour is planned.
4. Overnight stops should be thoroughly investigated.
5. Most travel agencies are reliable, but a personal investigation by a member or two from the senior group is recommended.
6. Details should be announced before and during the tour.
7. The cost of the entire tour should be known.
8. Particulars regarding meals, what meals will be included, should be announced.
9. Where the bus will pick up and what time the bus will leave is also important. Many older people have a tendency to worry about little things. The way they are seated, how they will get around, what they are to expect, are all of concern to them.
10. Those who drive, lead, and direct will do themselves a favor to be familiar with the needs of the older person, and the patience needed to lend an extra hand. Be willing to go the fourth, fifth, and sixth mile.
11. Many of the details as well as the decisions should be made by the older persons.
12. The leaders, or committee in charge, should be responsible for the plans and preparations.
13. The fees should all be handled by the older people themselves, thus along with the enjoyment, the obligations of touring are part of the total experience.

One group traveled to see a Christmas display in south Florida. Florida celebrates Christmas with lights instead of snow. The tour was totally arranged and planned by the senior group steering committee. The pastor happened to serve as the driver, but the pastor's only responsibility of the tour was driving the bus. A pleasant experience resulted from good publicity, personal contact by the leaders with those participating, arrangements for the meal, departure and return appropriate for the occasion. A good time was had by all.

Frequent bus tours can be learning adventures. Depending on your location, the sea and beach, the mountains and the countryside, museums, state parks, historical sites are always good educational adventures.

I. A committee conducted *a one day Convo-on-Aging* for Lutheran churches in a Midwest area.[2] Many county agencies happily provided speakers for the occasion. Films and literature regarding various services were made available. Everyone who attended agreed this was another pleasant method of "getting in on the know."

Another Fair on Aging was held on the campus of a local college and included a keynote address, entertainment, films on aging, and sharing of local programs.

J. Through *education* "older individuals can better adjust to changing life circumstances, become more stimulated and involved, and gain a greater sense of self-worth" (Academy for Educational Development, Inc., *Never Too Old to Learn*, June 1974, p. vii). This of course is another way of saying that self-satisfaction of the older person is a major key in ministering to, with, and by older people. As the senior citizen recognizes his self-satisfaction, he is putting into practice the "activity theory" which states, "there is a direct relationship of self-satisfaction to meaningful leisure-time experiences." Older people have two common experiences; loneliness and lack of purpose. If you discover these losses and deal with them, you will guarantee a successful ministry dealing with the basic needs of older people.

1. A Miami, Florida, congregation started a series of six meetings in their congregation entitled, "Partners Without Mates" for those over 55 years. Also available are educational courses related to losses of older people such as: Living Alone, Leisure Time, Finances, Employment, etc. All of these courses were taught by guest speakers from the respective fields.

2. Another related course offered in Florida to meet some of the needs of older persons is known as Pleasant Adventure Through Learning (PAL) which began as early as 1968. A stimulating and enriching program operates one morning a week from 9:30 a.m. to 12:30 p.m. for a series of 12 weeks. The range of subjects extends from religion, foreign nations, medicine, law, and ecology to scientific facts and life. The first hour relates to religion, the second hour to travel, and the third hour is devoted to a variety of topics. For all segments of the morning, volunteer speakers and films are acquired, with different individuals appearing on the program each week.

   Folks say, "It's the most meaningful activity in my life—the bright spot of my week—where I learn stimulating facts I can share with others." PAL means different things, but all agree it means a worthwhile morning. One talented person paraphrased a song for the group:

   "I love those dear hearts and gentle people,
       Who meet each Friday morn.
   We're PALS who travel—to foreign places,
       From Tokyo to Matterhorn.
   So much to learn, yet—it's a fun-day.
       Too fast, the morning goes.
   With those who stimulate discussions,
       They surely keep us on our toes.
   We feel so welcome each time that we return,
       At our coffee break no one is forlorn,
   I love those dear hearts and gentle people,
       The PALS who meet each Friday morn."

To keep your mind going, think about seminars,[3] afternoons, morning retreats. Include such topics or presentations as:

- Relating to your children
- Social Security Information
- Crimes Against the Elderly
- How to Make a Will
- Proper Nutrition
- Life Skills
- Investment Information
- Living on Fixed Incomes
- Community Affairs and Services
- Aging and the Bible
- Elderly Exercising
- Drug Abuse
- Medicare/Medicaid
- Law and the Senior Citizen
- Psychology and Aging
- Senior Adult Advocacy

There are a number of ready-made programs. Some of these are useful and you may want to examine them. Information is included in the Selected Resources, Bibliographical Data, of this manual. Just start asking your community service center, or call your local library, or write a letter to your denominational headquarters, and you will become familiar with many tested training programs.

ACTION/ACTIVITY SUGGESTIONS

Manuals like this help the most if the reader, through marginal notes and/or page markers, will key certain idea and case story areas in each chapter for action concentration. There is apt to be too much data, and it helps therefore to pick and choose and make your own outline for action from that material which applies most to you and your situation.

Why not, by a quick skimming right now, draw together your own "let's-get-going" outline? That way you will be getting involved in your own parish elderly ministry.

Chapter V

Addressing
Spiritual Concerns

Since this manual is concerned with engaging the aging in ministry in the church, it is appropriate to give some attention to specific methods and programs relating to spiritual concerns. One pastor decided to use the Bible class as a foundation for his ministry to, with, and by older people.[1] Here are some things he considered important:

A. *Designate a Sunday as a special occasion to highlight the needs and potentialities of older persons* within the congregation and the larger community. Such a special Sunday might include:

1. A special order of worship. A special Sunday bulletin prepared by NRTA (National Retired Teachers Association)—AARP is available to congregations without charge for use on a designated Sunday.
2. A sermon on "Overcoming Age Fright" or "Accept Your Age" or some other pertinent theme.
3. A discussion program in one or more adult classes on "The Role of Religion in the Later Years of Life" or other related topics.
4. A fellowship lunch for all members of the congregation. The program could feature presentations by the presidents of the local NRTA unit or AARP chapter, a film, or highlighting of contributions being made by older members both in the church and community. Be sure to include some refreshments, and you will automatically guarantee a good turnout.
5. A literature exhibit in the foyer or other location in your church including materials from the local library and NRTA-AARP. Pastors or other officials can order free literature from Church Relations Office, 1909 K Street, NW., Washington, DC 20049.

Special Worship and Spiritual Problems

Noteworthy differences in worship habits of senior citizens as compared with younger church members

Seniors seem to prefer the early hours for worship—leave the later service to the younger generation. Evening services are not always popular, although one must admire the faithfulness of those who attend Maundy Thursday or Good Friday evening Holy Communion services. The same applies to mid-week Lenten services. A few seniors get more concerned about their worship habits as they grow older, but, for the most part, golden-agers keep the habits they developed during their middle years. There are a fair percentage of "secret service" Christians in retirement communities. Then there are those who hide behind membership in the home congregation if they are currently living in another geographical area. Some are in the "cheerful giver" class, and some just don't find pleasure in giving to the Lord. Some feel pinched by the "tight" economy. Some widows truly give the "widow's mite." Seniors have a tendency to frown upon a great deal of change in worship habits. Many of them shy away from the guitar and contemporary music; they prefer the old liturgical paths to the new. Many elderly persons will enjoy a contemporary service for a change, but definitely prefer the customary order of worship. Attendance at worship services will usually drop if the seniors are fed too many contemporary worship forms. They are not too readily inclined to learn new hymn tunes and may even be irritated by innovations in the worship service. In a few exceptional cases senior citizens welcome change and seem to thrive on it. The wise pastor will learn to identify and serve the needs of the entire congregation, and this includes older persons.

There are a number of problems which the pastor will recognize as peculiar to older persons. Biological urges diminish as one gets older. Some senior citizens regard the waning of the sex urge as an indication of "overcoming the flesh," and feel they are becoming more sanctified. A 98-year-old shut-in remarked to her pastor, "Pastor, you don't have to bring the Lord's Supper to me so often." (He had been offering the Sacrament once every three months.) "I just sit here from day to day. I have no lust. In fact, I don't hate anyone." Fortunately, the pastor could correct her self-diagnosis by reminding her of an incident that occurred three months earlier when she had thrown her excretions at a nurse. Sometimes the aged have a tendency to forget the presence of original sin, the moments of anger, long-held grudges toward family and relatives, etc. All need the assurance of forgiveness, participation in the Lord's Supper, as well as a review of Christ's work of redemption as long as life goes on. Sins of omission are especially prevalent among senior citizens.

B. *Use Study and Discussion to Strengthen Faith, to Lessen Fears and Worries, and to Correct Religious Misconceptions.*

1. Topics may be formal or informal. Responses by the older persons are desired, and the good teacher or leader knows how important it is not to stifle reactions.

2. Do you want the hangups to surface? Then the teacher must have an attitude of tentativeness, a way of speaking which allows for discourse. The teacher must make it easy for the other person to come back with an objection—to say, "I don't quite understand what you mean." You must be scanning faces all the time, and sometimes you must stop long to sense the emotions that are going around and make it easy for people to come in with what they think and feel. You must spot resistance, invite response, and then carefully meet wrong notions with, "I can understand your point of view, but let's take a closer look at Scripture, etc." Don't clobber—you'll shut off feedback.

3. Older persons like to have the pastor lead the Bible class or religious topics. Many of them need the security of an able teacher and leader. Seniors are at the age when they don't want a great deal of argumentation on theological issues. They want to hear, "This is what God has to say to you in His Word."

4. Do you have a parochial school teacher or a good lay leader in your congregation who relates to this group? Alternate leadership. If you have Circle Bible Classes, ask others to alternate and of course, as usual, circumstances will always dictate your decisions.

Which methodology is most effective for Bible classes with older persons? Ordinarily pastor-led exegetical methodology is the most successful. The older person enjoys lecture-type lessons more than younger persons who want to become involved. Older people tire more easily than younger ones. The mental effort often leaves them sluggish. Topical Bible study seems to be appealing as a "change of pace," but even in that case, too great a dose will weaken Bible class and senior club attendance.

C. *Mature Adults Tend to Be Apprehensive in Learning Situations.*
The following are some potential causes of anxiety:
1. Older adults are sometimes fearful of revealing their ignorance. Great gaps exist in almost everyone's knowledge of the church and its dogma. Seniors are supposed to "know it all." After all, they have been exposed to a great deal of information. But many seniors hope they won't be called on or challenged by a fellow member to be specific at the wrong moment.
2. Being guilty of ignorance or misconception is not all that seniors dread; they also fear "letting the pastor down." They conceal their true feelings to spare him, because they respect him and what he stands for. This can be a praiseworthy impulse, but it can stand in the way of growth.
3. Older persons often fear to disagree. Let someone speak with authority and they "freeze." It causes pain to differ. So the older person protects himself with silence or by meekly nodding his head. They are especially hesitant to disagree with status persons. The Bible class or topic leader must therefore become skilled in developing a climate of freedom. When we become partners in learning with the class or group, we foster trust and security.
4. One clear barrier to the older person's learning is the built-in resistance to change. Many older people want to remain just as they are. Our basic tendency to resist change is not necessarily bad or good. It is part of our nature. It enables us to maintain stability in the word which surrounds us. We must remember that resistance to change is normal; we should expect it and welcome it. An individual without this resistance may be scatter-brained and disoriented.

D. *You Can Expect Change After the Need for Change Is Recognized.*
1. The leader can help the class understand the fact of resistance to change.
2. How much training does the leader need to involve older people actively in the learning process?
3. The key to the problem lies in the ability to relate to people. Ask yourself: "What kind of a person are you? What is your total package like."

Some Suggestions for Bible Study and Discussion

A. The Bible—Various Versions, How It Came to Be, etc.
B. Topical Courses—Heaven, Hell, Worry, Sin, Faith, Divine Promises, Forgiveness, etc.
C. Discussion Courses—How About Prayer? What About the End of the World? How to Combat Loneliness, etc.
D. Exegetical Courses—Books of the Bible, Early Church according to Acts. Various titles include, *Is Yours a Living Faith?* (James). *Doing Things Decently and in Order* (1 and 2 Corinthians). *The Gospel by a Man Named Mark* (Mark), etc.

E. *Devotions.* Devotions are integral for opening or closing meetings of clubs, organizations, or retreats. As you prepare these devotions, keep in mind that older people enjoy singing, praying, and reading Scripture. Arrange for senior participation. Special poems read by members of the group may be encouraged. Short meditations by a capable senior will be enjoyed. (Check Appendix A for Biblical references.)

Variety Can Spice Up Prayer Lives Too

One congregation holds successful annual parish twilight retreats—sometimes for a single night, at other times, for as many as three nights in a row.

Once the focus was on the realities and special concerns of our aging years; another time it involved very contemporary problems such as alcoholism, divorce, and the single parenting problems; and still another session concentrated on death and dying, and on living with grief and widowed loneliness.

What appeared to be most significant in these very human ministries was that persons learned that they were not the first, nor the only, people who had ever suffered their particular sadnesses or circumstances.

ACTION/ACTIVITY SUGGESTIONS

Special Resource Information

St. Mary's College Press, of Winona, MN, offers a comprehensive loose-leaf-type system called: PACE 10. This data includes specific home visitation, nursing home and hospital visitation advice, and sample training dialogs, plus evangelization questions with suggested answers. It appears to have broad Christian usefulness. The material, which may be duplicated as much as desired, is most thorough and useful. The present editor is Mary Perkins Rine. Contacting this press for a review copy, or more detailed literature, might be a practical way to assure yourself that the material is appropriate to your own particular parish use.

In addition to this material, you will find in the bibliographic section at the back of this manual many other useful books, films, and other media materials with which you can create a modest shelf for yourself and your committee to draw from to get your own aging ministry under way.

Chapter VI

Special Information for Clergy

Since one of the prime people involved in ministering to, with, and by older people is the pastor, the following information is offered to encourage, enlist, and enlighten clergy. Numerous workshops and other types of presentations have developed materials which have been tested and tried to meet the needs of older people. Many pastors give scant attention to social, physical, or emotional needs of the older person. Some ministers, some educational leaders, as well as some religious authorities have attempted to express the church's concern in the field of gerontology. They all are agreed that "religion is the natural agency for older people to turn to, and for older people to expect help from in time of need."

Here are some of the growing number of developments in the concern of the church for the aging:

The National Interfaith Coalition on Aging, Inc. (NICA) suggested various innovative models for gerontological training of clergy and lay leaders. Some of the models presented at the August 1979 meeting held in Indianapolis included:

1. *Pilot Design for Pastor Training,* J. Russell Hale, Lutheran Theological Seminary

   A pilot project for a series of 1979—80 regional "seminars on Ministry to Aging," under the auspices of the Lutheran Council in the U.S.A. Designed with staff assistance of the Institute of Gerontology (University of Michigan), the seminars involved 5,060 Lutheran pastors in 12 locations for 8 sessions of intensive didactic/experimental learning in plenary, small-group, and dyadic input/ discussion settings.

2. *The Role of the Congregation in Ministry with/to Older Persons,* William F. Case, St. Paul School of Theology, Kansas City, MO.

   This workshop is designed to equip a team from a congregation to develop and implement a ministry with and to older persons. A congregation contracts to send a team of three or four persons to the workshop and agrees for this team to enter into a learning contract which involves preparation for participation in the workshop and followthrough after the workshop.

3. *The Church's Unique Role in Aging,* Margaret Sanford—Synod of Albany (RCA), Ronald Sanford—New Brunswick Theological Seminary.

   Most clergy and lay leaders are aware of the great need for ministry with the elderly. However, they often do not know how to minister to the elderly and what resources are available to help them fulfill their spiritual well-being.

4. *Aging: A Local Church Ministry,* Rex. D. Wilson, consulting pastor for the Benton Neighborhood Program for the Elderly, Benton, Ill.
Easy-to-understand and easy-to-use tools for the local church in its development of a ministry, to, for, and with the aging. Consciousness-arousing attitude and stereotype studies, needs, and available services considered.

5. *Seminars on Ministry with the Aging,* Donald F. Clingan, Executive Director Department of Services to Congregations, National Benevolent Association of the Christian Church (Disciples of Christ), Indianapolis, Ind.
One of the greatest challenges facing congregations of all faiths is sensitive, effective ministry with the aging, enabling older persons to give of their full potential to church/synagog and society. This model, designed for training clergy and lay leaders, seeks to enable participants to—

    A. build within themselves and others a new concept of aging;

    B. help congregations begin an effective ministry with the aging;

    C. implement the unique roles of congregations in ministry with the aging (including direct emphasis on the spiritual well-being of the elderly).

Literally a host of workshops, seminars, retreats, and conferences are available for heightening pastoral skills in ministering to and with the older person. Official newsletters and other informational materials announce various presentations offered throughout the country. There is a serious concern on the part of churches to offer a ministry to, with, and by the older person. There are special concerns, contentions, and commitments needed on the part of pastors and leaders of the church. The bottom line is clear: "Inasmuch as ye have done it unto one of the least of these My brethren, ye have done it unto Me" (Matthew 25:40). Perhaps even more specific is the cry of the elderly in Psalm 71:9, "Do not cast me off in the time of old age; forsake me not when my strength is spent" (RSV).

ACTION/ACTIVITY SUGGESTIONS

Each minister, of whatever denomination, will also probably have in his library or otherwise at his disposal a great deal of good and useful material—much of it may be denominational, diocesan, or synodical in its nature. Or it may have been prepared specially for those who labor in your particular vineyard.

Now is the time to draw all of this material together and to use its values to help you build your own special parish ministry for your own aging. Use any guidelines, but make it your own program so that you and your members can feel comfortable and at home with it. What you will want is the acceptable action, that which is manageable in your congregation and its special circumstance.

Notes

Chapter II—How to Administer a Senior Ministry

1. Keith, Pat M. "Perceptions of Needs of aged by Ministers and the Elderly," *Review of Religious Research,* 18 (Spring 1977), 278—82.
2. The Shepherd Center; 5144 Oak St., Kansas City, MO.

Chapter III—Socialization Needs and Opportunities

1. Many ideas have been investigated and results are available from *Aging,* by Tom. E. Prevost. This is a Handbook on Aging and Senior Adult Ministries sponsored by the Home Mission Board, Southern Baptist Convention, Atlanta, Georgia.

Chapter IV—Education and Older Persons

1. *From Care and Counseling of the Aging,* William M. Clements, Fortress Press, 1979.
2. Many of the ideas presented in this chapter are from the study made by the Florida Lutheran Task Group on Aging, a joint ministry of The American Lutheran Church, the Lutheran Church in America, and The Lutheran Church—Missouri Synod.
3. A good example of seminars relative to aging is the Midwest Workshop on Ministry with Aging Persons in the Community of Faith. Anderson School of Theology, Anderson, Ind.

Chapter V—Addressing Spiritual Concerns

1. From an unpublished paper, "Bible Class and the Golden Age," Dr. Paul A. Lassanske at Institute for Adult Bible Studies, Concordia Theological Seminary, Fort Wayne, Ind., June 1978.

Appendix A

SCRIPTURE REFERENCES TO OLD AGE

Psalm 71:9—Do not cast me off in the time of old age; forsake me not when my strength is spent.

Proverbs 20:29—The glory of young men is their strength, but the beauty of old men is their gray hair.

Proverbs 16:31—A hoary head is a crown of glory; it is gained in a righteous life.

Isaiah 46:4—Even to your old age I am He, and to gray hairs I will carry you. I have made, and I will bear; I will carry and will save.

Deuteronomy 34:7—Moses was a hundred and twenty years old when he died; his eye was not dim, nor his natural force abated.

Job 5:25-26—You shall know also that your descendants shall be many, and your offspring as the grass of the earth. You shall come to your grave in ripe old age, as a shock of grain comes up to the threshing floor in its season.

Psalm 91:14-16—Because he cleaves to me in love, I will deliver him; I will protect him . . . . I will be with him in trouble, I will rescue him and honor him. With long life I will satisfy him, and show him My salvation.

Proverbs 10:27—The fear of the Lord prolongs life, but the years of the wicked will be short.

Leviticus 19:32—You shall rise up before the hoary head, and honor the face of an old man, and you shall fear your God; I am the Lord.

From the Revised Standard Version of the Bible, copyrighted 1946, 1952, © 1971, 1973. Used by permission.

Ecclesiastes 12:1-8—Remember also your Creator in the days of your youth, before the evil days come, and the years draw nigh, when you will say, "I have no pleasure in them"; before the sun and the light and the moon and the stars are darkened and the clouds return after the rain; in the day when the keepers of the house tremble, and the strong men are bent, and the grinders cease because they are few, and those that look through the windows are dimmed . . . when the sound of the grinding is low, and one rises up at the voice of a bird, and all the daughters of song are brought low; they are afraid also of what is high, and terrors are in the way, the almond tree blossoms, the grasshopper drags itself along and desire fails; because man goes to his eternal home, and the mourners go about the streets; before the silver cord is snapped, or the golden bowl is broken, or the pitcher is broken at the fountain, or the wheel broken at the cistern, and the dust returns to the earth at it was, and the spirit returns to God who gave it. Vanity of vanities, says the Preacher; all is vanity.

On Longevity

Genesis 5:4—The days of Adam after he became the father of Seth were eight hundred years, and he had other sons and daughters.

V. 8—Thus all the days of Seth were nine hundred and twelve years, and he died.

V. 11—Thus all the days of Enosh were nine hundred and five years, and he died.

V. 14—Thus all the days of Kenan were nine hundred and ten years, and he died.

V. 17—Thus all the days of Mahalalel were eight hundred and ninety-five years; and he died.

V. 20—Thus all the days of Jared were nine hundred and sixty-two years, and he died.

V. 31—Thus all the days of Lamech were seven hundred and seventy-seven years, and he died.

Genesis 9:29—All all the days of Noah were nine hundred and fifty years, and he died.

Genesis 11:11—And Shem lived after the birth of Arpachshad five hundred years, and had other sons and daughters.

Genesis 25:7—These are the days of the years of Abraham's life, a hundred and seventy-five years.

Deuteronomy 31.2—And he said to them, "I am a hundred and twenty years old this day; I am no longer able to go out and come in. The Lord has said to me, 'You shall not go over this Jordan.' "

Joshua 24:29—After these things Joshua the son of Nun, the servant of the Lord, died, being a hundred and ten years old.

1 Samuel 4:15—Now Eli was ninety-eight years old and his eyes were set, so that he could not see.

1 Samuel 12:2—And now, behold, the king walks before you; and I am old and gray, and behold, my sons are with you, and I have walked before you from my youth until this day.

2 Samuel 19:35—I am this day eighty years old; can I discern what is pleasant and what is not? Can your servant taste what he eats or what he drinks? Can I listen to the voice of singing men and singing women? Why then should your servant be an added burden to my lord the king?

1 Chronicles 29:28—Then he David died in a good old age, full of days, riches, and honor; and Solomon his son reigned in his stead.

Job 42:17—And Job died, an old man, and full of days.

Psalm 92:12-15—The righteous flourish like the palm tree, and grow like a cedar in Lebanon. They are planted in the house of the Lord, they flourish in the courts of our God. They still bring forth fruit in old age, they are ever full of sap and green, to show that the Lord is upright; He is my Rock and there is no unrighteousness in Him.

1 Peter 3:10—For "He that would love live and see good days, let him keep his tongue from evil and his lips from speaking guile."

Old Testament References to Old Age

Exodus 20:12—Honor your father and your mother, that your days may be long in the land which the Lord your God gives you.

Deuteronomy 5:33—You shall walk in all the way which the Lord your God has commanded you, that you may live, and that it may go well with you, and that you may live long in the land which you shall possess.

Deuteronomy 11:21—That your days and the days of your children may be multiplied in the land which the Lord swore to your fathers to give them, as long as the heavens are above the earth.

1 Kings 3:14—And if you will walk in My ways, keeping My statutes and My commandments, as your father David walked, then I will lengthen your days.

Psalm 91:16—With long life I will satisfy him, and show him My salvation.

Isaiah 65:21-22—They shall build houses and inhabit them; they shall plant vineyards and eat their fruit. They shall not build and another inhabit; they shall not plant and another eat; for like the days of a tree shall the days of My people be, and My chosen shall long enjoy the work of their hands.

Zechariah 8:4—Thus says the Lord of hosts: Old men and old women shall again sit in the streets of Jerusalem, each with staff in hand for very age.

Genesis 15:15—As for yourself, you shall go to your fathers in peace; you shall be buried in a good old age.

Ecclesiastes 11:1—Cast your bread upon the waters, for you will find it after many days.

Feebleness in Old Age

1 Kings 1:1—Now King David was old and advanced in years; and although they covered him with clothes, he could not get warm.

Ecclesiastes 12:3—. . . in the day when the keepers of the house tremble, and the strong men are bent, and the grinders cease because they are few, and those that look through the windows are dimmed

Ecclesiastes 12:5—They are afraid also of what is high, and terrors are in the way; the almond tree blossoms, the grasshopper drags itself along and desire fails; because man goes to his eternal home, and the mourners go about the streets

Zechariah 8:4—Thus says the Lord of hosts: Old men and old women shall again sit in the streets of Jerusalem, each with staff in hand for very age.

Gray Hair

Job 15:10—Both the gray-haired and the aged are among us, older than your father.

Proverbs 16:31—A hoary head is a crown of glory; it is gained in a righteous life.

Proverbs 20:29—The glory of young men is their strength, but the beauty of old men is their gray hair.

Hosea 7:9—Aliens devour his strength, and he knows it not; gray hairs are sprinkled upon him and he knows it not.

Dimness of Vision

Genesis 27:1—When Isaac was old and his eyes were dim so that he could not see, he called Esau his older son and said to him, "My son"; and he answered, "Here I am."

Genesis 48:10—Now the eyes of Israel were dim with age, so that he could not see. So Joseph brought them near him; and he kissed them and embraced them.

1 Samuel 3:2—At that time Eli, whose eyesight had begun to grow dim, so that he could not see, was lying down in his own place

1 Samuel 4:15—Now Eli was ninety-eight years old and his eyes were set, so that he could not see.

Ecclesiastes 12:3—. . . in the day when the keepers of the house tremble, and the strong men are bent, and the grinders cease because they are few, and those that look through the windows are dimmed.

Reverence for Old Age

Leviticus 19:32—You shall rise up before the hoary head, and honor the face of an old man, and you shall fear your God. I am the Lord.

Job 32:6—And Elihu the son of Barachel the Buzite answered: "I am young in years, and you are aged; therefore I was timid and afraid to declare my opinion to you."

Proverbs 23:22—Harken to your father who begot you, and do not despise your mother when she is old.

New Testament References

Luke 1:5-25—In the days of Herod, king of Judea, there was a priest named Zechariah, of the division of Abijah; and he had a wife of the daughters of Aaron, and her name was Elizabeth. And they were both righteous before God, walking in all the commandments and ordinance of the Lord blameless. But they had no child, because Elizabeth was barren, and both were advanced in years.

Now while he was serving as priest before God when his division was on duty, according to the custom of the priesthood, it fell to him by lot to enter the temple of the Lord and burn incense. And the whole multitude of the people were praying outside at the hour of incense. And there appeared to him an angel of the Lord standing on the right side of the altar of incense. And Zechariah was troubled when he saw him, and fear fell upon him. But the angel said to him, "Do not be afraid, Zechariah, for your prayer is heard, and your wife Elizabeth will bear you a son, and you shall call his name John. And you will have joy and gladness, and many will rejoice at his birth; for he will be great before the Lord, and he shall drink no wine nor strong drink, and he will be filled with the Holy Spirit, even from his mother's womb. And he will turn many of the sons of Israel to the Lord their God, and he will go before him in the spirit and power of Elijah, to turn the hearts of the fathers to the children, and the disobedient to the wisdom of the just, to make ready for the Lord a people prepared." And Zechariah said to the angel, "How shall I know this? For I am an old man, and my wife is advanced in years." And the angel answered him, "I am Gabriel, who stand in the presence of God; and I was sent to speak to you, and to bring you that good news. And behold, you will be silent and unable to speak until the day that these things come to pass, because you did not believe my words, which will be fulfilled in their time." And the people were waiting for Zechariah, and they wondered at his delay in the temple. And when he came out, he could not speak to them, and they perceived that he had seen a vision in the temple, and he made signs to them and remained dumb. And when his time of service was ended, he went to his home. After these days his wife Elizabeth conceived, and for five months she hid herself, saying, "Thus the Lord has done to me in the days when He looked on me, to take away my reproach among men."

Luke 1:57-80—Now the time came for Elizabeth to be delivered, and she gave birth to a son. And her neighbors and kinsfolk heard that the Lord had shown great mercy to her, and they rejoiced with her. And on the eighth day they came to circumcise the child; and they would have named him Zechariah after his father, but his mother said, "Not so; he shall be called John." And they said to her, "None of your kindred is called by this name." And they made signs to his father, inquiring what he would have him called. And he asked for a writing tablet, and wrote, "His name is John." And they all marveled. And immediately his mouth was opened and his tongue loosed, and he spoke, blessing God. And fear came on all their neighbors. And all these things were talked about through all the hill country of Judea; and all who heard them laid them up in their hearts, saying, "What then will this child be?" For the hand of the Lord was with him. And his father Zechariah was filled with the Holy Spirit, and prophesied, saying:

"Blessed by the Lord God of Israel, for He has visited and redeemed His people, and has raised up a horn of salvation for us in the house of His servant David, as He spoke by the mouth of His holy prophets from of old, that we should be saved from our enemies, and from the hand of all who hate us; to perform the mercy promised to our fathers, and to remember His holy covenant, the oath which He swore to our father Abraham, to grant us that we, being delivered from the hand of our enemies, might serve Him without fear, in holiness and righteousness before Him all the days of our life. And you, child, will be called the prophet of the Most High; for you will go before the Lord to prepare His ways, to give knowledge of salvation to His people in the forgiveness of their sins, through the tender mercy of our God, when the day shall dawn upon us from on high to give light to those who sit in darkness and in the shadow of death, to guide our feet into the way of peace."

And the child grew and became strong in spirit, and he was in the wilderness till the day of his manifestation of Israel.

Luke 2:22-35—And when the time came for their purification according to the law of Moses, they brought Him up to Jerusalem to present Him to the Lord (as it is written in the law of the Lord, "Every male that opens the womb shall be called holy to the Lord") and to offer a sacrifice according to what is said in the law of the Lord, "a pair of turtledoves, or two young pigeons." Now there was a man in Jerusalem, whose name was Simeon, and this man was righteous and devout, looking for the consolation of Israel, and the Holy Spirit was upon him. And it had been revealed to him by the Holy Spirit that he should not see death before he had seen the Lord's Christ. And inspired by the Spirit he came into the temple; and when the parents brought in the Child Jesus, to do for Him according to the custom of the law, he took Him up in his arms and blessed God and said, "Lord, now lettest Thou Thy servant depart in peace, according to Thy word; for mine eyes have seen Thy salvation which

Thou hast prepared in the presence of all peoples, a light for revelation to the Gentiles, and for glory to Thy people Israel."

And His father and His mother marveled at what was said about Him; and Simeon blessed them and said to Mary His mother, "Behold, this Child is set for the fall and rising of many in Israel, and for a sign that is spoken against (and a sword will pierce through your own soul also), that thoughts out of many hearts may be revealed."

Luke 2:36-38—And there was a prophetess, Anna, the daughter of Phanuel, of the tribe of Asher; she was of great age, having lived with her husband seven years from her virginity, and as a widow till she was eighty-four.... And coming up at that very hour, she gave thanks to God and spoke of Him to all who were looking for the redemption of Jerusalem.

1 Timothy 5:1-4—Do not rebuke an older man but exhort him as you would a father; treat younger men like brothers, older women like mothers, younger women like sisters, in all purity. Honor widows who are real widows. If a widow has children or grandchildren, let them first learn religious duty to their own family and make some return to their parents; for this is acceptable in the sight of God.

Hebrews 11:21—By faith Jacob, when dying, blessed each of the sons of Joseph, bowing in worship over the hand of his staff.

Titus 2:2-3—Bid the older men be temperate, serious, sensible, sound in faith, in love, and in steadfastness. Bid the older woman likewise to be reverent in behavior, not to be slanderers or slaves to drink; they are to teach what is good.

Appendix B

Bible Study

Some Attitudes Toward the Elderly and the Aging Process

1. Read Genesis 27:1-40
   a. What gives Isaac the right to decide which son shall be the primary heir?
   b. What were the symptoms of Isaac's old age?
   c. How would you describe Jacob's attitude toward Rebekah's plan?
   d. How might Rebekah have justified her trickery?
   e. How did you feel towards Jacob for defrauding Isaac?
   f. What made even Isaac's mistaken placement of birthright legal and binding?
   g. What attitudes towards Isaac made Esau the loser?
2. Read Genesis 42:1-38
   a. How does Jacob provide for the family's survival in famine?
   b. What attitude of his sons towards an elderly father is necessary?
   c. What does Jacob feel would be the result of his grief if evil should befall Benjamin?
   d. How do the sons respond to this fear?
3. Read Genesis 46:28-30
   a. What is Joseph's attitude toward the elderly Jacob?
   b. What is Jacob's attitude toward death at this point?
4. Read Genesis 47:7-12
   a. Does Jacob seem to feel that he has lived an average span of life?
   b. What does Jacob feel has shortened his span of life?
   c. Do you feel that our attitudes towards trouble affect the length of our life? have some other consequences/of such attitudes.
5. Read Genesis 48:1-22
   a. Is Jacob's word as an elderly man now considered law?
   b. What physical failing of old age does Jacob display?
   c. What is Joseph's initial reaction to Jacob's "error" in blessing the second son as if he were the firstborn?
   d. To what does Joseph attribute this error?
   e. Why did Jacob do it? . . . as possibly a self-justification of the way he received his own birthright?
   f. Is an older man's word, even though contrary to custom, now accepted as law?
   g. What do you feel might have prompted Jacob to recommend the family's continued identification with certain Canaanite lands?

Application of New Testament Values to Attitudes Toward the Elderly and the Aging Process

1. Read Matthew 15:1-9
   a. The Value: The "korban" as an economic, human tradition defies the law of God as expressed in the Fourth Commandment.

b. Question: What economic values do we have, if any, that defy "righteous" attitudes and practices towards elderly people?

2. Read Luke 5:27-32
   a. The Value: Those who realize their need for help are receptive to and appreciative of help and healing, especially spiritual help.
   b. Question: Are our elderly members (and "inactive" members) receptive and appreciative of the church's ministries that are really helpful to them? Is this any different from the response of the other age groups? Are the elderly more realistic about their needs?

3. Read Luke 7:36-50
   a. The Value: One who knows himself to be forgiven much, or many times, tends to be more loving, tolerant, compassionate.
   b. Question: Does a person who has lived through many situations in life, and who realizes how many times he or she depended upon mercy, tend to be more loving, tolerant, and compassionate? Would there be some value to the church gained by providing more exposure of these people to people not as spiritually mature?

4. Read Luke 8:26-39
   a. The Value: One who experiences a great deal of spiritual comforting can be commissioned to witness to what God has done for him.
   b. Question: How can the great resource of experienced persons who can look back and see the things that God has done for them over the years be tapped for evangelism and outreach in the church?

5. Read Luke 17:11-19
   a. The Value: One person can refuse to be so self-centered and preoccupied with the expectations of "the Law" that he can share spontaneous gratitude in response to God's mercy.
   b. Question: One of the advantages of aging and retiring is sometimes a liberation of the attitudes from the demands of "the Law." Have we appreciated this liberation among our elderly to the extent that we can encourage spontaneous expression of it?

Appendix C

A PLAN OF ACTION TO ACHIEVE A GOAL

1. What do we want to accomplish? (One specific goal)

2. What is the target date for achieving our goal?

3. The steps we will take to reach our target date. (Time line)

By _____ we will _____.

By _____ we will _____.

By _____ we will _____.

4. What resources are needed?

Money: Personnel:

Talent: Other:

5. Who will do what by when?

	Person	*Task*	*By When*
a.			
b.			
c.			
d.			

6. When and how will we evaluate our achievements?

Appendix D

GOAL EVALUATION SHEET*

THE OBJECTIVE _____

_____

TARGET DATE: _____

TIME LINE:

     BY (date) _____ WE ACCOMPLISHED _____ .

     BY (date) _____ WE ACCOMPLISHED _____ .

     BY (date) _____ WE ACCOMPLISHED _____ .

WHAT IT COST:

     MONEY: We spent _____ for _____ .

     PERSONNEL: These persons were involved _____ .

     Other: We used _____ TO FULFILL OUR OBJECTIVE.

WHOSE NEEDS WERE MET:

WHAT CHANGES WE MIGHT MAKE IF WE WERE TO DO IT AGAIN:

HOW IMPORTANT WAS MEETING THIS OBJECTIVE IN RELATION TO
OUR GENERAL STATEMENT OF PURPOSE?

*To help the group improve its effectiveness, compare the Plan of Action sheet
dates and assignments with what really happened. What does this say?

Appendix E

SAMPLE ENLISTMENT FORM

INFORMATION CARD

SUNSHINE	A	Peace Lutheran Church-1901 E.
SENIOR	CHRISTIAN	Commercial Boulevard,
CITIZENS	COMMUNITY	Ft. Lauderdale, Fla.—33308
SOCIETY	CAUSE	

Your Name—Mr. Mrs. Miss

Are you a visitor?   Yes   No

Local Address

Church Membership

City, State, and Zip

Are you new in the area? Yes No

Phone Number

Do you have transportation needs?

Your Birthday—Year Optional

Place of Birth, Your Option

Moved to Florida From

This form is intended to get to know you better. You may supply any information you desire. It is not intended as a mailing list.

On the reverse side you may indicate any special talents, interests, hobbies, musical or oratorical interests, and any comments you wish to make.

Appendix F

LEE NEEDS ASSESSMENT SURVEY

Name _____ Phone _____ Age _____

Address _____ Male _____ Female _____

Married _____ Widow/er _____ Single _____

LIVING ARRANGEMENTS: With Children _____ With Other

Relatives _____ Alone _____

LIVE IN: Home _____ Apartment _____ One Room _____ Group

Facility _____

Able to Leave Home Freely _____ Unable to Leave Home _____

Able to Leave Home with Assistance _____

HEALTH: Good _____ Fair _____ Poor _____

SPECIFIC HEALTH CONCERNS:

DISABILITY: Vision _____ Hearing _____ Mobility _____ Other _____

EMPLOYMENT: Full Time _____ Part Time _____ Retired _____

Never Employed Outside Home _____ (former) Occupation _____

Hobbies and Recreational Preferences: _____

_____

Special Skills or Academic Interests: _____

_____

(over)

[back]

SPECIFIC NEEDS AND INTERESTS

SERVICES IN THE HOME   X=Services Needed   O=Services I Can Give

_____ Cooking   _____ Crafts & Hobbies   _____ Minister's Visit

_____ Shopping   _____ Nursing Care   _____ Letter Writing

_____ Lawn Work   _____ Minor Repairs   _____ Daily Telephone
                                                        Check

_____ Snow Removal (?) _____ Friendly Visits _____ Live-in
                                                         Companion

_____ Emergency Contact (any kind) _____ Trusted Person to Confide In

Other Services Needed _____

_____

SERVICES AWAY FROM HOME

EMPLOYMENT: Full Time _____ Part Time _____ Retired _____

TRANSPORTATION TO AND FROM: Doctor's Office _____ Store _____

Church _____ Hospital _____ Other _____

I CAN PROVIDE TRANSPORTATION: Times: _____

VOLUNTEER INTERESTS

I would be interested in information on opportunities to help other people:

From My Home _____   Their Home _____   In the Community _____

Bibliographical Data

A. SELECTED RESOURCES

Action
806 Connecticut Ave. NW.
Washington, DC 20525
An independent federal agency with three administrative areas, head-quarters in Washington, with 10 regional offices. Programs: Foster Grandparent Program; Retired Senior Volunteer Program; and Senior Companion Program.

Action for Independent Maturity
1909 K St. NW.
Washington, DC 20049
A division of the American Association of Retired Persons, with special programs and emphasis for persons age 50 to 65. Excellent resource for literature and course materials for preparing beforehand for a fuller retirement living experience. Publishes *Dynamic Years* magazine, available only to members.

American Association of Homes for the Aging
1050 17th St. NW., Suite 770
Washington, DC 20036
A resource for anyone wishing special knowledge about health care cost and legislation about Medicare and Medicaid reforms; special emphasis on activities and services, and on research and training programs.

American Association of Retired Persons
1909 K St., NW.
Washington, DC 20049
Over 11 million members; with interest and concerns about legislative programs, lobbying for the older person; publishers of instructional and advisory materials, and of *Modern Maturity* magazine, available only to members. Prime movers behind causes of the retired and elderly.

American Society of Mature Catholics
1100 West Wells St.
Milwaukee, WI 53233
Publishers of the bimonthly magazine *Mature Catholic;* a nonprofit group in its second decade of service dedicated to the spiritual and economic welfare of Catholics age 50 and over.

B'nai B'rith International
1640 Rhode Island Ave., NW.
Washington, DC 20036
A community volunteer organization providing tax counseling and available benefits information for older Americans; with visiting seniors in institutions and assisting the elderly who live alone as primary service concerns.

Central Bureau for the Jewish Aged
225 Park Ave. South
New York, NY 10003
Coordinating group serving the New York Metropolitan Jewish Community; maintains Jewish homes for the aged, hospitals, community centers, and camps for the aged.

National Council on the Aging
1828 L St. NW.
Washington, DC 20036
Private, nonprofit organization serving as a national resource for research, planning, information, technical consultation, and publications relating to older persons; with some special emphasis on guiding the growth and development of senior centers across the nation; plus many and varied pilot-testing programs.

New England Gerontology Center
15 Garrison Ave.
Durham, NH 03824
Elderhostel program. Continuing education available on hundreds of college and university campuses.

Retirement Advisors, Inc.
720 Fifth Ave.
New York, NY 10019
One of the very first, this commercial organization provides services and informational programs to individuals and organizations on all matters concerning retirement.

Tell-The Institute for Enrichment of Later Life
1600 South Minnesota
Sioux Falls, SD 57105
A commercial organization emphasizing projects, programs, materials—with a special spiritual thrust—for those who wish to mount their own local activity affairs for enriching the lives of older persons; for better understanding aging.

SPECIAL MENTION

Aid Association for Lutherans
Appleton, WI 54911
The Family Health Section of AAL's Fraternal Affairs Division has

created and is presenting on a national basis within the Lutheran Church community a preretirement series of study sessions called S.M.A.R.T.— Senior Members and Retirees Training. Very worth knowing about.

Chicago Catholic Archdiocese
Catholic Charities Service for Senior Citizens
721 North LaSalle St.
Chicago, IL 60610
As just one among an increasing number of church bodies, this staff-and-volunteer program embodies many useful parts. They have an umbrella group called Senior Senate; they publish a monthly *Keen-Ager News* which delineates ongoing projects, programs, and informational data to guide and encourage pastors, parish councils and committees, parish pastoral assistants, and other staff and volunteer persons in what can and is being accomplished in this vital heartland diocese, for the elderly or those approaching that time of life.

Lutheran Brotherhood
701 Second Avenue South
Minneapolis, MN 55402
What LB calls "a contribution to Lutheran congregations through their national church offices . . . from Lutheran Brotherhood . . . a fraternal benefit society, is what has come to be known as LEE (Life Enrichment for the Elderly.") This program is the result of an "active study with responsible planning to support our aging population." This guiding concept ought to be better known.

The American Lutheran Church
Division for Service and Mission in America
422 South Fifth St.
Minneapolis, MN 55415
"Changing Aging"—A congregational resource on aging, designed to generate workshops that help congregations broaden and deepen opportunities for growing—both the "aged" and the "aging." A good place to start.

U.S. Office of Human Development Services
Special Programs for the Aging
U.S. Department of Health and Welfare
400 6th Street, SW.
Donahoe Building
Washington, DC 20201
Includes the national Administration on Aging, principal governmental body through which information and programs implementing the Older Americans Act are communicated and managed; the Office serves as an advocate within HEW for the needs of aging groups.

Institute on Religion and Aging
1100 West 42nd St.
Indianapolis, IN 46208

Interfaith Council for Family Financial Planning
   277 Park Ave.
   New York, NY 10017

International Society of Preretirement Planners
   P.O. Box 1137
   Omaha, NE 68101

The National Interfaith Coalition on Aging, Inc.
   298 South Hull St.
   Athens, GA 30601

SPECIALIZED MAGAZINES FOR RETIREMENT AND AGING
Aging
   Department of Health and Welfare
   Washington, DC 20201

Dynamic Years
   1909 K St., NW.
   Washington, DC 20049

50-PLUS Magazine
   850 Third Ave.
   New York, NY 10022

Modern Maturity
   215 Long Beach Blvd.,
   Long Beach, CA 90801

B. MEDIA SOURCES

"Age-Related Vision and Hearing Changes—An Empathic Approach" (Slide/Tape)
   A two-part production (110 slides with audio cassette narrative). Part 1 provides basic information on normal age-related sensory changes; Part 2 simulates the experience of functioning with these vision and hearing changes.

"Nobody Ever Died of Old Age" (16 mm Film)
   Dramatizes the lives of a series of independently resourceful older citizens who are struggling to survive and retain some measure of dignity. Film combines praise for older people with outrage at the dehumanization they experience. Based on the book by Sharon Curtin, *Henry Street Settlement.*
   Films Incorporated
   733 Green Bay Rd.
   Wilmette, IL 60091

"One More Winter" (16 mm Film)
  A poignant vignette of an old couple's romance which generates envy in a blase young man, as yet untouched by love. Written and directed by Francoise Sagan.
  Films Incorporated (see address above)

"Volunteer to Live" (16 mm Film)
  A documentary filmed at the Shepherd's Center in Kansas City, the film outlines self-help projects offering opportunities for the elderly to aid themselves and others. A program of the Central United Methodist Church under the direction of Rev. Dr. Elbert Cole, it can serve as a model project for ways in which churches can become involved in working with the elderly.
  TV Film Library
  Room 860
  475 Riverside Dr.
  New York, NY 10027

"The Wild Goose" (16 mm Film)
  This film views the life of a vital, mischievous old man who is confined in an environment where he doesn't belong—a nursing home. The scenes are short vignettes of nursing home life. The dull, drab, sterile life, where people are treated like babies, without dignity, is contrasted to this spirited man—the wild goose.
  Films Incorporated (see address above)

"What Is Successful Aging? Part 1 (Slide/Tape)
  Examines the aging process in terms of its biological, psychological, social, and chronological components. Delineates the changes that occur as people age and demonstrates that while some of these changes indicate decline, others reflect growth and development.

"What Is Successful Aging?" Part 2 (Slide/Tape)
  Discusses and evaluates various sociopsychological approaches such as disengagement theory, activity theory, adaptive tasks, and personality theory, which attempt to explain how successful aging can be achieved. Explains a method of measuring life-satisfaction and describes three different but equally successful patterns of aging.
  CONCEPT MEDIA
  P.O. Box 19542
  Irvine, CA 92714

"Who Am I? Am I Still a Person?" A Nursing Home Dialog (Slide/Tape)
  Illustrated by cartoons on slides, this training unit interprets familiar institutional situations from the perspectives of the administrator of a nursing home and an elderly resident of the home.
  Institute of Gerontology
  Ann Arbor, MI

Simulations

"Brookside Manor" (Simulation)

> A leader's manual and instruction units for a simulation dramatizing the needs of elderly people who leave their own homes for institutional life. Designed for 30 to play, it has also been used effectively for groups of 16 to 60.
> Institute of Gerontology
> Ann Arbor, MI

"Retirement Options: A Gerontological Simulation" (in development)

> This simulation provides a forum for discussion about a prospective retiree's options with regard to living arrangements, use of time, and relationships with others. It explores feelings, attitudes, and ideas concerning retirement options from the points of view of the older person and of an adult child. Designed for use with intergenerational families, students, and family counselors.
> Institute of Gerontology
> Ann Arbor, MI

"Taking a Chance on the Later Years" (Simulation Game)

> An educational tool in card game format, this simulation is designed to dramatize for those working with the elderly the impact of life losses upon the lives of older people.
> Institute of Gerontology
> Ann Arbor, MI

C. KEY BOOKS AND ARTICLES

Anderson, Margaret J. *Looking Ahead.* St. Louis: Concordia Publishing House, 1978.

———— *Your Aging Parents.* St. Louis: Concordia Publishing House, 1979.

Ankenbrandt, T. F. "Church and Mature Christians," *America,* 135 (Nov. 13, 1976), 318—19.

Arnold, Oren. *Guide Yourself Through Old Age.* Philadelphia: Fortress Press, 1976.

Asquith, Glenn H. *Living Creatively as an Older Adult.* Scottdale, PA: Herald Press, 1975.

Arthur, Julietta K. *Retire to Action.* Nashville, TN: Abingdon Press, 1969.

Forbes, C. A. "Old and Ugly: Never," *Christianity Today,* 16 (April 14, 1972), 40—41.

Gould, Elaine, and Loren Gould. *Crafts for the Elderly.* Springfield, IL: Charles C. Thomas, 1971.

Hopping, B. "Conversations in the Waiting Room for Death," *Nursing Homes,* 25 (Nov. 1976), 18—20.

Kalish, Richard A. *Late Adulthood: Perspectives on Human Development.* Monterey, CA: Brooks/Cole Publishing Company, 1975.

————. *The Later Years, Social Applications of Gerontology.* Monterey, CA: Brooks/Cole Publishing Company, 1977.

Kerr, Horace L. *How to Minister to Senior Adults in Your Church.* Nashville, TN: Broadman Press, 1980.

Lahey, M. "Aging's Gift: Freedom," *New Catholic World,* 216 (July 1973), 166—70.

McClellan, Robert W. *Claiming a Frontier: Ministry and Older People.* Los Angeles: The University of Southern California Press, 1977.

Merrill, Toni. *Discussion Topics for Oldsters in Nursing Homes: 365 Things to Talk About.* Springfield, IL: Charles C. Thomas, 1974.

Morgan, C. "Seniors Step Forward: Senior Citizen Tutoring Program for Problem Learners. Redding, CT" *American Education,* 11 (November 1975), 6—9.

Neugarten, Bernice L. *Middle Age and Aging: A Reader in Social Psychology.* Chicago and London: The University of Chicago Press, 1968.

NICA issues bulletin to assist churches in meeting elderly's needs. Aging, 243 (January 1975): 15.

Otte, Elmer. *Preretirement Planning System.* Appleton, WI: Retirement Research, 1975.

————. *Rehearse Before Your Retire.* Appleton, WI: Retirement Research, 1977.

————. *Welcome Retirement.* St. Louis: Concordia Publishing House, 1974.

Parker, Pamela L., ed. *Understanding Aging.* Philadelphia: United Church Press, 1974.

Parker, Florence E. *Care of the Aged Persons in the United States.* New York: Arno Press, 1976.

Robertson, Josephine. *Prayers for the Later Years.* Nashville, TN: Abingdon Press, 1972.

Rossow, Irving. *Socialization to Old Age.* Los Angeles: University of Southern California Press, 1975.

Sinick, Daniel. *Counselling Older Persons: Careers, Retirement, Dying.* New York and London: Human Sciences Press, 1977.

Vickery, Florence E. *Creative Programming for Older Adults: A Leadership Training Guidebook.* New York: Association Press, 1972.

Wandress, J., and M. Kohn. "Retirees Should Be Recycled for Public-Interest Work," *Retirment Living,* 15 (December 1975), 40—42.

D. AN ANNOTATED BIBLIOGRAPHY ON AGING IN CATEGORIES

Prepared by
   Dr. Donald F. Clingan, Executive Director
   Department of Services to Congregations
   The National Benevolent Association of the Christian Church
   (Disciples of Christ)
   P.O. Box 1986
   Indianapolis, IN 46206

Note: The following resources in the field of aging represent a collection made from many religious bodies and are believed to be particularly helpful to congregations of all faiths seeking to develop and implement a "ministry with the aging."

ON UNDERSTANDING AGING

Aging and Mental Health: Positive Psychosocial Approaches.
Robert N. Butler and Myrna I. Lewis. The C. V. Mosby Company, St. Louis, 1973.
Excellent on the nature and problems of old age and evaluation, treatment, and prevention.

Aging Is Not for Sissies. Terry Schuckman. The Westminster Press, Philadelphia, PA, 1975.
Excellent on building a better concept of aging and its potentialities.

Aging: The Fulfillment of Life. Henri J. M. Nouwen and Walter J. Gaffney. Doubleday and Company, Inc., Garden City, NY., 1974, $6.95.
A beautiful book in pictures and prose dealing with aging as a way to the darkness and light, and caring as a way to the self and to the other.

A Time to Enjoy: The Pleasures of Aging. Lillian R. Dangott and Richard A. Kalish. Prentice-Hall, Inc., Englewood Cliffs, NJ 07632, 1979.
Includes chapters on The Potential of Aging, Myths of Aging, Aging: A Time for Opening to New Experiences, Prevention of Physical Deterioration, Choosing Health Habits, Mind and Body Living Together: Staying Healthy, Developmental Tasks and Aging, and The Pleasures of Aging.

Claiming a Frontier: Ministry and Older People. Robert W. McClellan. University of Southern California Press, Los Angeles, CA, 1977.
Excellent guidelines, understanding the new task of ministering to older persons in our congregations.

Fact Book on Aging: A Profile of America's Older Population. Charles S. Harris. Published by The National Council on the Aging, Inc., 1828 L Street, NW., Washington, DC 20036, February 1978.
Includes information on demography, income, employment, physical health, mental health, housing, transportation, criminal victimization of the aging.

Facts and Myths About Aging. A booklet published by The National Council on the Aging, Inc., 1828 L Street NW., Washington, DC 20036.
Includes information on the myth, the facts about aging in brief and simple form.

Live All Your Life. Reuel L. Howe, Word Books, Publisher, Waco, TX, May 1976 (Revised).
Stresses the perspective of staying younger while growing older, and the pilgrimage from birth to life. Beautiful concepts of aging with a theological base.

Sensitizing People to the Processes of Aging: The Inservice Educator's Guide. Marvin Ernst and Herbert Shore. Published by the Center for Studies in Aging, School of Community Services, North Texas State University, Denton, TX, May 1976.
Includes chapters on Vision, Hearing, Touch, Dexterity, Taste, Smell, and Mobility and Balance.

The Black Elderly: A Guide for Practitioners. Joseph Dancy, Jr. Published by The Institute of Gerontology, The University of Michigan—Wayne State University, 520 East Liberty Street, Ann Arbor, MI 48109, 1977.
Includes sections on Society's View: The Elderly and Elderly Blacks, The Black Elderly and the Major Problems of Aging, and A Profile of the Black Elderly.

The Fourth Generation: A Call for New Understanding and Care for the Growing Numbers Over Age 75. John M. Mason, Augsburg Publishing House, Minneapolis, MN, 1978.
Includes chapters on The Dilemna of Old Age, The Changing Family, Problems Facing the Elderly, Warehouses for the Living Dead, Voiceless Victims of Exploitation, Behind the Scenes with Bureaucrats, Case Histories of Failure, Suffocation by Regulation, Voices Raised in Warning, and Houses of Healing and Love.

The Myth and Reality of Aging in America. A Study for The National Council on the Aging, Inc., by Louis Harris and Associates, Inc., April 1975. Order from The National Council on the Aging, Inc., 1828 L. Street, NW., Washington, DC 20036.
An excellent resource to fight the myths of aging and build a new concept of growing older. Research within the study is most valuable.

Toward a Theology of Aging. Seward Hiltner, Editor. Human Sciences Press, New York, NY 1975.
Printed lectures given at a conference on the Theology of Aging sponsored by the National Retired Teachers Association/American Association of Retired Persons during the spring of 1974. The lectures consider in an ecumenical context the implications of theology for older persons and for the ways we think about the aging process. One of the few books published in this field.

Why Survive? Being Old in America. Robert N. Butler, M.C. A Pulitzer Prize winner. Harper and Row, Publishers, New York, NY, 1975.
An outstanding and comprehensive book in the field of aging.

ON PRERETIREMENT

Add Years to Your Life and Life to Your Years. Dr. Irene Gore. Stein and Day, Publishers, New York, NY, 1975.
Contains some practical suggestions on how to make aging special.

Mandatory Retirement: Present Practices and Directions and the Search for More Just and Humane Alternatives. Dr. Donald F. Clingan. December 1977. Order from National Benevolent Association, Dept. of Services to Congregations, P.O. Box 1986, Indianapolis, IN 46206. $4.00
A doctoral research study paper.

Plan Now for Your Retirement: Free to Do, Free to Be. Published by Retirement Services Incorporated, P.O. Box 5325, Eugene, OR 97405.

An excellent packet with booklets on the following subjects: "Retirement: Dreams, Doubts, Strategies," "Aging: Old Myths versus New Facts," "Financial Planning: A Positive Approach to Living Within Your Means," "Thinking About Where You Will Live," "Activities: Free to Do, Free to Be," "Your Relationships with Other People," "Personal Health Management: Be Your Body's Best Friend," "Peace of Mind: Achieving the Vital Balance," "A Fresh Look at Yourself: Your Most Important Resource," and "Self-Fulfillment: A Lifelong Challenge."

Series on Retirement: Ethel Percy Andrus Gerontology Center, 1974:
Nutrition for Health and Enjoyment in Retirement
Is My Mind Slipping?
What About the Generation Gap?
Available from the Publications Office, Andrus Gerontology Center, University of Southern California, University Park, Los Angeles, CA, 90007.

The Bright Years, How to Make Your Retirement the Best Time of Your Life. Sam C. Reeves. Fleming H. Revell Company, Old Tappan, NJ, 1977.
The title tells the purpose of this book.

The Later Years Can Be the Greater Years. Published by Kiwanis International, 101 East Erie Street, Chicago, IL 60611.
A booklet dealing with attitudes, finances, health, housing, time, consumer fraud, the law, and programs and services in the last years.

Welcome Retirement. Elmer Otte, Concordia Publishing House. St. Louis, MO, 1974.
This little book helps those facing retirement to deal with the serious questions in this stage of life. The author calls upon future retirees to "rehearse retirement living" rather than to make retiring a "surprise party."

ON DEATH AND DYING

AIM's Guide to Single Living, published by Action for Independent Maturity, A division of American Association of Retired Persons, 1909 K Street, NW., Washington, DC 20049.
Includes information on housing, credit, single lifestyles, tips for entertaining on your own, financial planning, and travel.

Caring for the Grieving. C. Earl Gibbs. Omega Books, Corte Madera, CA, 1976.
Includes chapters on Avoidance of Death, Philosophical and Religious Orientation to Death, The Dying Patient, The Experience of Grief, The Meaning and Value of Funerals, and Beyond Professionalism.

Death, Dying, Grief and Funerals. Richard J. Obershaw. Grief Center, 318 Riverwoods Lane, Burnsville, MN 55337, 1976.
Includes sections on death in our society today, dying in our society today, grief and bereavement, the funeralization process, children and death, funeralization cost, things to do at time of death.

Developing a Widowed Services Program, Hazel M. Foss and Frances G. Scott. 1977. Order from Widowed Services Program, University of Oregon, 1643 Agate Street, Eugene, OR 97403. $3.00 per copy.
Includes sections on why a widowed services program, how to establish a widowed services program, service components of a model program, the clients of a widowed services program, reprise and recommendations, and a comprehensive appendix.

Dialogue with Death, Abraham Schmitt. Word Books, Publisher, Waco, TX, 1976. Helps a person face death from the "gut-level" in a beautiful perceptive and concise way.

Hospice: Creating New Models of Care for the Terminally Ill. Parker Rossman, Association Press, New York, NY, 1977. $9.95
Includes chapters on Mrs. Morgan Wanted to Die at Home, The Dilemma of the Family, Health-Care Professionals and the Dying, The Hospice Concept in England, The New Haven Hospice: An American Adaption, Challenges and Alternatives, The Hospice Concept as Program, Advice to Other Communities, Some Financial Aspects, and Home Care for the Dying.

Living with Dying. Glen W. Davidson. Augsburg Publishing House, Minneapolis, MN, 55415, 1975.
Includes chapters on What Does Dying Mean? When Dying Means Loss, When Dying Means Change, When Dying Means Conflict, When Dying Means Suffering, and When Dying Means Triumph. Along with the basic book, a study guide is available.

The Dying Person and the Family. Nancy Doyle. Public Affairs Pamphlet No. 485, Public Affairs Pamphlets, 361 Park Ave. South, New York, NY 10016. 50¢ per copy.
Concise, to the point, and extremely helpful on facing death and dying. Includes key sections on the five emotional states of dying, anticipatory grief, how children see death, and helping the family.

The Finishing Touch. Marion Osborn. 1976. Order from national Benevolent Association, Dept. of Services to Congregations, P.O. Box 1986, Indianapolis, IN 46206. 50¢ per copy.
Rituals, customs, and laws when death comes.

To Live Until We Say Goodbye. Elisabeth Kubler-Ross and Mal Warshaw. Prentice-Hall, Inc., Englewood Cliffs, NJ, 1978. $12.95.
Beautiful pictures and perceptive prose on the stages of death of actual persons and on alternatives to hospital care.

Widows and Widowhood: A Creative Approach to Being Alone. James A. Peterson and Michael L. Briley. Association Press, New York, NY, 1977.
The title tells the purpose of this book.

ON CREATIVE EDUCATION

A Matter of Life and Death. Shirley J. Heckman. A youth Elect Series unit for older youth produced by and for the churches participating in Christian Education: Shared Approaches (CE:SA), 1978. Available from Christian Board of Publications, Box 179, St. Louis, MO 63166.
Excellent curriculum. Sessions on "Why Do People Have To Die?" "Is Taking of Human Life Ever Justified?" "How Can I Live When I Know I'm Dying?" "How Can I Deal with Grief?" and "How Do We Relate to Matters of Life and Death in a Christian Sense?"

Care and Counselling of the Aging. William M. Clements. Fortress Press, Philadelphia, PA, 1979. $2.95.
Includes chapters on Getting in Touch with Aging, Time and the Illusion of Age, Developmental Crisis, Reminiscence, and Completing the Task.

In Wisdom and the Spirit: A Religious Education Program for Those Over Sixty-five. Sara and Richard Reichert. Paulist Press, New York, NY, 1976.
Includes five units: "The Phenomenon of Aging," "Priesthood of the Elderly," "Prayer and Spiritual Life," "Reconciliation and Eucharist," and "Death, Dying and Resurrection." Also includes a section on suggested craft projects.

Maggie Kuhn on Aging. A Dialogue Edited by Dieter Hessel. The Westminster Press, Philadelphia, PA, 1977.
Though there are some glaring inaccuracies to those who know the field of aging in this book, its content deserves serious consideration by congregations of all faiths. Action is the key word!

Survival Handbook for Children of Aging Parents. Dr. Arthur N. Schwartz. Follett Publishing Company, Chicago, IL 1977. $6.95.
Includes information on growing old, senility, retirement, institutionalization, alternative living, death and dying, how you are not on your own.

The Church's Ministry with Older Adults: A Theological Basis. Martin J. Heinecken and Ralph R. Hellerich. A study book issued by the Consulting Committee on Aging, Division for Mission in North America, Lutheran Church in America, 231 Madison Avenue, New York, NY 10016, 1976.
Includes three parts: "The Church's Ministry with Older Adults: A Theological Basis," "Guide for Study and Discussion," and on the "Consulting Committee on Aging."

Understanding Aging. Pamela Parker, Editor. The United Church Press, 287 Park Avenue South, New York, NY 10010, 1974.
A Shalom Resource for use with 10 to 14-year-olds. Includes four units of one of four sessions. Excellent.

ON CONGREGATIONS AND AGING

Aging Persons in the Community of Faith. Dr. Donald F. Clingan. 1975. Order from National Benevolent Association, Dept. of Services to Congregations,

P.O. Box 1986, Indianapolis, IN 46206. $1.00 plus 50¢ postage.
A guidebook for churches and synagogues on ministry to, for, and with the aging.

Because We Care: How to Organize a Lay Ministry with Shut-ins. Thomas Walker. 1977. Order from Service Center, Board of Global Ministries, 7820 Reading Rd., Cincinnati OH 45237. $1.50 per copy.
Excellent guidebook prepared for the Health and Welfare Ministries Division by the Education and Cultivation Division Board of Global Ministries. The United Methodist Church.

Claiming a Frontier: Ministry and Older People. Robert W. McClellan. 1977. Order from Publications Office, Andrus Gerontology Center, University of Southern California, University Park, Los Angeles, CA 90007. $3.50 plus 35¢ postage.
An excellent guidebook in ministry with the aging written out of the rich experience of the author in a model congregational ministry at the Chatsworth Adult Center, Point Loma Community Presbyterian Church, San Diego, CA.

Continuing Choices. Published by the National Council of Jewish Women, One West 46th Street, New York, NY 10036. $21.00 per copy.
A 49-page handbook of programs for and with the aging. Very comprehensive. Concise.

Does Anybody Care? A Guide for Visiting in Nursing Homes. Mary R. Ebinger. Order from Manorcare, 10080 Lockwood Drive, Silver Spring, MD 20901.
A most helpful guidebook on understanding the patient, understanding the nursing home, and suggested visiting procedures.

Enlarge Your World. Ways Senior Adults Can Assert—and Enjoy—Themselves in Community Life. John Warren Steen. Broadman Press, Nashville, TN, 1978. $2.50.
The title and subtitle are very descriptive of the purpose of this book.

It's Good to Have a Friend! Ruth Baker, 1970. Order from Age Center of Worcester Area, Inc., 025 Worcester Center, MA 01608.
The best guidebook one could have for developing a program of friendly visiting with the aging.

I Was Sick and You Visited Me. Mary R. Ebinger, Women's Division, Board of Global Ministries, The United Methodist Church. Order from Service Center, Board of Global Ministries, 7820 Reading Road, Cincinnati, OH 45237. 35¢ per copy.
An excellent guidebook designed to increase the skills and insights of the visitor and to create a better understanding by the visitor of various types of patients and their needs.

Instruction Manual on the Older Adult Church Survey Project. David L. Batzka. Order from National Benevolent Association, Dept. of Services to Congregations, P.O. Box 1986, Indianapolis, IN 46206. $1.00 plus 50¢ postage.

Includes complete instructions and guidelines for the survey process; three sample tools for the survey of congregational members 55 years of age and older through a random sample, the Community Social Services survey, and the Church Program Survey; and explanation of the method for developing a random sample of congregational members; guidelines for the Interview Process, including an Interviewer's Training Manual; guidelines on the Older Adults Planning Procedure; and an explanation on the Tabulation of Data from the Three Surveys.

Let Your Light Shine! A Research Study Measuring the Impact of One-Day Older Adult Retreats and a Twelve-Week Small-Group Experience on Older Persons, by Dr. Donald F. Clingan. Order from National Benevolent Association, Dept. of Services to Congregations, P.O. Box 1986, Indianapolis, IN 46206. $15.00 plus $1.50 postage.
A doctoral field project-in-ministry. 255 pages.

Life Enrichment for the Elderly: A Lutheran Handbook. Published by the Lutheran Brotherhood, 701 Second Avenue South, Minneapolis, MN 55402.
Chapters included on What are the Elderly like? What are Our Goals? How Do We Begin? What Can We Do? and What are Our Resources?

Manual to Assist Congregations in Their Ministry with the Elderly. Published by the Presbytery of Philadelphia, Church and Community Committee, Subcommittee on Ministry with Older Adults, Revised December 1977. Order from Presbytery of Philadelphia, Department of Church and Community, 2200 Locust Street, Philadelphia, PA 19103. 50¢ per copy PREPAID.
Manual stresses needs of older persons and how congregations can help with these needs.

Mission Action Group Guide: The Aging. A guide for mission action group members to use in ministering and witnessing to the aging. Published by Woman's Missionary Union (Southern Baptist Convention), 600 North Twentieth Street, Birmingham, AL 35203, 1969, 1972.

Mission Action Group Guide: The Sick. A guide for mission action group members to use in ministering and witnessing to the sick. Published by Woman's Missionary Union (Southern Baptist Convention), 600 North Twentieth Street, Birmingham, AL 35203, 1967.

"Old but Full of Sap." Rev. Donald E. Crismon. Order from National Benevolent Association, Dept. of Services to Congregations, P.O. Box 1986, Indianapolis, IN 46206. 50¢ plus 25¢ postage.
Institute on Religion and Aging 1978 Award Winning Sermon

Project Compassion, A Program to Involve Lutheran Christians in Sharing Christ and Self with Troubled People, The Lutheran Church—Missouri Synod, The Board of Social Ministry and World Relief, 500 N. Broadway St. Louis, MO 63103.
A training packet for "friendly visitor" volunteers serving in nursing homes, homes for the aging, general hospitals, prisons, mental health institutions.

Project: Head II (Help Elderly Adult Direct) Victorina A. Peralta. Order from National Benevolent Association, Dept. of Services to Congregations, P.O. Box 1986, Indianapolis, IN 46206. $1.00 per copy.
  A self-help formula by the City of Philadelphia for mobilizing churches/ synagogues in social action neighborhood-based program with the elderly.

The Church and the Older Person. Robert M. Gray and David O. Moberg. William B. Eerdmans Publishing Company, 255 Jefferson Avenue, SE., Grand Rapids, MI 49503. Revised Edition, 1977.
  Includes chapters on the problems of older people, the religion of older people, religion and personal adjustment in old age, personal adjustment of the older person within the church, contribution of the church to adjustment, problems of the older person in the church, what the church can do for older people, what older persons can do for the church, and the clergy and older people.

The Grandbook of Programs for the Aging. James A. Hayeland. Twenty-Third Publications, P.O. Box 180, West Mystic, CT 06388, 1978. $9.95.
  Includes: An overview, why should the church care, why does the government care, how we can care, and resources.

What Churches Can Do for Senior Adults. A pamphlet published by The South Carolina Commission on Aging, 915 Main St. Columbia, SC 29201.
  An excellent pamphlet describing specific types of needed ministry with older adults.

ON COMMUNITY AND AGING

A Guide to Intergenerational Programming. Bella Jacobs, Pat Lindsley, and Mimi Feil. Published by the National Institute of Senior Centers, a Program Unit of the National Council on the Aging, Inc., 1828 L Street, NW., Washington, DC. 20036, February 1976.
  This publication offers program suggestions and a training guide for Senior Center directors or other skilled group workers to prepare youth volunteers to work effectively in activities which bring youth and older persons together.

Citizens Action Guide: Nursing Home Reform. Prepared by Elma Griesel and Linda Horn for The Gray Panthers, 3700 Chestnut Street, Philadelphia, PA 19104, Third Printing March 1976. $3.00 per copy. Checks payable to the Gray Panthers.
  Includes information on the problems, actions taken by consumer groups and others interested in long-term care reform, recommendations for action, necessary preliminary work, planning for action and community support, and recommendations for specific actions to be initiated, supported, or conducted by citizen groups and voluntary organizations.

Crime Prevention Handbook for Senior Citizens. Julie Edgerton. Published by Midwest Research Institute, 425 Volker Boulevard, Kansas City, MO 64110.
  Includes chapters on How Vulnerable Are You? How to Reduce the Odds

of Being the Victim of a Burglary, How to Reduce the Odds of Being the Victim of a Robbery or Larceny, and How to Reduce the Odds of Being the Victim of a Fraud.

Exercises While You Watch TV Third Printing, August, 1977. Order from Sickroom Services, Inc., 2534 S. Kinnickinnic Avenue, Milwaukee, WI. $1.25 per copy.

Guidelines for Chapters in Providing Volunteer Services for and by the *Visually Handicapped.* No. 2 in the Program Guidelines Series; *Friendly Visitor Services*, No. 7 in the Program Guidelines Series; *Telephone Reassurance Service*, No. 8 in the Program Guidelines Series. Published by The American National Red Cross, Washington, DC, 1973.
One-page, concise guidelines for the development of services.

Guidelines for a Telephone Reassurance Service. Virginia Rogers. DHEW Publication No. (OHD) 75-20200. Order from Superintendent of Documents, U.S. Government Printing Office, Washington, DC 20402.
Gives excellent information on how to develop a telephone reassurance service.

Involving Men: A Challenge for Senior Centers. Bella Jacobs. Published by the National Institute of Senior Centers, a Program Unit of the National Council on the Aging, Inc., 1928 L Street, NW., Washington, DC 20036, March 1974.
Includes information on the problem, special concerns of older men, the senior-center image, barriers to participation, motivating men to participate, target program for men; ideas, resources, examples.

Recommended Standards and Guidelines for Agencies Providing In-Home Services. Prepared by the NVOILA Quality In-Home and Supportive Services Subcommittee. Jointly produced by the National Voluntary Organizations for Independent Living for the Aging, a Program of The National Council on the Aging, Inc., 1828 L Street, NW., Washington, DC 20036, and the National Division and the Women's Division of the Board of Global Ministries of The United Methodist Church.
Order from the National Council on the Aging, Inc. $1.00 per copy.

S O S 11: Developing Day Care for Older People. Helen Psdula. Published by The National Council on the Aging, Inc., 1828 L Street, NW., Washington, DC 20036, September 1972.
Includes information on definitions, target population, program, transportation, size, hours, physical standards staffing, records, evaluation, and how to begin planning.

S O S 17: Advocacy in the Field of Aging. Jack Leff. Published by the National Council on the Aging, Inc., 1828 L Street, NW., Washington, DC 20036, October 1972.
Includes assessment of needs of the elderly, elders' role in policymaking, programs in operation, relations with other agencies.